MEDITATIONS *for* MEETINGS

---

*Thoughtful Meditations
for Board Meetings
and for Leaders*

---

collected by EDGAR STOESZ

Good Books

Intercourse, PA 17534
800/762-7171

Dedicated to the memory of
WILLIAM T. SNYDER
Friend
Mentor
Servant Leader

Acknowledgments

Those biblical citations given as "NRSV" are from the *New Revised Standard Version Bible*, © 1989 by the Division of Christian Education of the National Council of the Churches of Christ in the United States of America. Used by permission.

Those biblical citations given as "RSV" are from the *Revised Standard Version of the Bible*, © 1946, 1952, 1971 by the Division of Christian Education of the National Council of the Churches of Christ in the United States of America. Used by permission.

Those biblical citations given as "NIV" are from the *Holy Bible, New International Version*, © 1973, 1978, 1984 by the International Bible Society. Used by permission of Zondervan Bible Publishers.

Those biblical citations given as "KJV" are from the *King James Version of the Bible.*

Those biblical citations given as "NKJV" are from the *New King James Version of the Bible*, © 1979, 1980, 1982 by Thomas Nelson, Inc. Used by permission.

Those biblical citations given as "TLB" are from *The Living Bible*, © 1971. Used by permission of Tyndale House Publishers, Inc., Wheaton, IL 60189. All rights reserved.

Design by Dawn J. Ranck

MEDITATIONS FOR MEETINGS
Copyright © 1999 by Good Books, Intercourse, PA 17534
International Standard Book Number: 1-56148-244-7
Library of Congress Catalog Card Number: 98-53690

Library of Congress Cataloging-in-Data Publication
Meditations for meetings : thoughtful meditations for board meetings
and for leaders / collected by Edgar Stoesz.
p. cm.
Includes index.
ISBN: 1-56148-244-7
1. Meetings--Prayer-books and devotions--English. 2. Church com-
mittees--Prayer-books and devotions--English. I. Stoesz, Edgar.
BV4596.C49M43 1999
242'.68--dc21   98-53690
                                                      CIP

Table of Contents

Note: The meditations are arranged alphabetically by the writers' last names.

An Index listing the meditations by themes appears on page 181.

About *Meditations for Meetings*

Many board and committee meetings start with a meditation of some sort, or at least a prayer. This includes the U. S. Congress and even professional athletic games. Many of these moments, however, are little more than a pause to permit the meeting to settle down so the official business can begin. That is not good enough. Here is an opportunity to create a spiritual environment that will permeate the meeting and influence the decision-making process.

Meditations for Meetings is intended to help make God's presence felt in the board room. Many boards include members who can lead a meaningful devotional. Others boards do not. Some board members who believe in prayer do not feel comfortable praying publicly. **Meditations for Meetings** is designed to assist in all those circumstances.

This book contains 77 meditations written by 56 persons, an international collection of men and women. They are executives, teachers, and ministers. No single writer could produce such variety. Thank you for writing so forthrightly and with such spiritual depth.

Two esteemed friends helped me make the final selection of pieces in this collection—Lynette Meck and Myron Ebersole.

I also gratefully acknowledge the editing work of Phyllis Pellman Good in making the book more readable, while retaining the writers' meanings.

I have included 44 prayers with which the Rev. James David Ford, D.D., Chaplain, opened sessions of the U.S. House of Representatives. My grandson Matthew Bauman helped select the prayers.

Each prayer has a brief title indicating its character or theme. Use from this collection in settings or occasions when a prayer without a meditation is appropriate, or when you prefer one of these prayers to those included with individual meditations.

This book may be used in numerous ways. It is primarily intended for those times of reflection at the beginning of board or committee meetings. It may also be used to lead in small group worship.

Use the Index of themes (page 181) to select a meditation suitable for your particular meeting. Mix the meditation with silence; be free to expand or adapt readings to fit your group.

Leaders may want to use **Meditations for Meetings** for their own devotions, to gain Divine perspective on their role.

Ministers may find it to be a rich resource of illustrations and human interest stories.

May all your work be blessed.

—**Edgar Stoesz, Akron, Pennsylvania**

And the Meditation
of my Heart

*"Let the words of my mouth and the meditation of
my heart be acceptable to you, O Lord, my rock and
my redeemer."*

— Psalm 19:14 (NRSV)

The overhead light in my office was retrofitted several
years ago so that it automatically comes on when I enter
the room and automatically shuts off when I leave. The
light is sensitive to movement. It stays on as long as there is
activity in the room. One problem is that occasionally the light
goes off when I am in the room . . . when I am quietly reading
or thinking. The light "assumes" there is no activity in the room
when motion ceases. It counts only physical activity as evidence
of human presence in the room.

Board meetings are similar. They consist primarily of people
talking. When talk stops, we tend to assume that activity has
stopped and that it is time to take action—to vote, to table, to
move on to the next issue. We seem to believe that persons are
active only when they are talking. I have been at meetings
where an individual (usually one who has already made his or
her point several times) will say, "Well, no one else is talking so
I will," as if talking is all that matters. There seems to be no
room for the internal activities of thinking, meditating, or
reflecting on an issue.

I do not recall being part of a board meeting where an issue was
raised and we were given time to think about it before responding.
Normally the question is asked and the talking begins, unless the
group is too large and the members do not know one another.

Perhaps everyone feels pressed for time. Meetings are typically packed into a day and a half or two days, and there are too many items on the agenda. But boards should recognize that not all of the activity in the room is in the talk. Some of the activity is taking place in the silence. It would be wise for boards to pause and allow members to reflect, meditate, think, and pray from time to time, particularly before taking actions.

May both the words of our mouths and the meditations of our hearts be acceptable in your sight, O Lord, our rock and our redeemer. Amen.

Some activity may be taking place in the silence.

— **Wilma Ann Bailey, Grantham, Pennsylvania**

Character or Reputation?

"Whatever happens, conduct yourselves in a manner worthy of the gospel of Christ. Then . . . I will know that you stand firm in one spirit . . . for the faith of the gospel."

— Philippians 1:27 (NIV)

"Finally, beloved, whatever is true, whatever is honorable, whatever is just, whatever is pure, whatever is pleasing, whatever is commendable, if there is any excellence and if there is anything worthy of praise, think about these things."

— Philippians 4:8 (NRSV)

How we respond to good and evil reflects our faith and determines our destiny.

During my early and mid-teens I had a lively Sunday school teacher. He saw character as what we *really* are deep down inside when no one is looking. In contrast, he believed that reputation is what others *think* we are, which often is somewhat different! My teacher had the habit of asking direct questions—what would Jesus say about how you treat your family, care for animals, drive the car, earn or spend money, play or talk about your neighbors?

I had a high school teacher who made current events and history come to life. He was also my basketball coach and taught me much about playing fair, respecting my body, being part of a team, and having fun.

I was fortunate. These two teachers gave me a way to grade my character during the week and, along with my parents, were very important in shaping my life. Later, Charles Sheldon's book, *In His Steps,* challenged me in decision-making to always ask, "What would Jesus do in this situation?"

Character means standing up for what we believe is right, and doing that with grace and humility. This is not an easy task. Daily we face pressures to cut corners. We may be tempted to put on our most righteous faces and to hide our character cracks. Often our characters weaken internally before any external patterns show. If we stumble, as all of us do at times, let us accept responsibility, seek forgiveness, and get back on our bicycles again. Inner peace and joy come only as we truly live our convictions.

Rejoice. God is at work in us. God offers unrationed grace. Power lines connect us to God's grace. We are "members one of another." Jesus in John 16:33 reassures us, "I have said this to you so that in me you may have peace. In the world you face trouble. But take courage; I have overcome the world."

Thank you, God, for your amazing, unrationed grace. Let it penetrate our souls. Help us find and follow Jesus' way. Strengthen our characters. *Amen.*

"It is in solitude that we discover that being is more important than having and that we are worth more than the results of our efforts. In solitude we discover that our life is not a possession to be defended but a gift to be shared." —Henri Nouwen

— Atlee Beechy, Goshen, Indiana

Facing Crisis

"Have I not commanded you? Be strong and coura-
geous. Do not be terrified; do not be discouraged, for
the Lord your God will be with you wherever you go."
— Joshua 1:9 (NIV)

How does a crisis feel? Your throat turns to cotton. You wonder if others hear the blood pulsing through your heart as it races to your brain. A rush of adrenaline leaves you momentarily stunned. You experience denial: This cannot be happening—not here, not to me, not to my organization, not now. Reality overpowers denial. The TV cameras are coming and a reporter is in the lobby. It is real, it is terrifying, and it is happening! The question is how will I respond?

Several years ago the Ashland Oil Company discovered their oil tanks were leaking into a major river. The river was the central water supply for the surrounding towns. John Hall, the CEO, faced a barrage of difficult choices. He could blame it on something or someone. He could say, "No comment." He could deny it was their problem. He could acknowledge the failure of the company. John Hall decided to accept responsibility for the problem. While realizing his company's vulnerability, he chose courage over caution or deception. At the moment when he was most tempted to deny what was happening, he found people to be the most forgiving.

Joshua of the Old Testament also faced difficult choices. Moses had died and they had not yet gained the Promised Land. He suddenly found himself in the middle of a leadership crisis. Like John Hall, Joshua did not accept the advice of those who urged caution. Instead, he acknowledged his problem, he faced discouragement, he risked failure, and moved forward. The people of Israel supported honest leadership making a difficult decision.

This is a reality of organizational life—you will face crisis and painful choices. Leaders make very public decisions. Organizations become dysfunctional. Do not look for ways to "spin" the problem. Do not blame it on the "devils's hand" or past leadership. Do not allow counselors to convince you that the problem is elsewhere. Regardless how embarrassing, own the problem and carry on. When being honest, directors can put the organization on the road to recovery and find renewed support. Faith to make difficult decisions makes a great deal of difference.

We acknowledge our shortcomings and failures. Give us the courage to embrace crisis as an opportunity for growth and understanding. Give us faith to make difficult decisions. Thank you for the strength to move forward. Amen.

Oil spills create a slippery mix; courageous response to crisis should not.

— **Curt Bechler, North Newton, Kansas**

Consider Each Other

"But if God so clothes the grass of the field, which is alive today and tomorrow is thrown into the oven, will he not much more clothe you—you of little faith? Therefore do not worry, saying, 'What will we eat?' or 'What will we drink?' or 'What will we wear?' For it is the Gentiles who strive for all those things; and indeed your heavenly father knows that you need all these things."

— Matthew 6:30-32 (NRSV)

We had been in Choma, Zambia for five days and had not yet eaten a single meal in our new home. What a display of hospitality on the part of our fellow missionaries! They were careful to attend to our physical needs which, when we first arrived, overpowered most of our spiritual needs. We were dumbfounded at their warm greetings. They backed up their friendly words with kind actions and tangible expressions of concern.

Such hospitality reminded me of Old Testament times, when caring for someone's physical needs was a responsibility of the entire community. The New Testament practices continued along these same lines. During Jesus' earthly ministry, he demonstrated concern for the whole person; he saw physical healing and forgiveness of sins as two sides of the same coin.

When we come as board members to a meeting, we bring our whole selves, not just brains to think and mouths to discuss. But do our personal needs so preoccupy us that we are distracted from the agenda? Sometimes it is useful to build time into the agenda to get acquainted, even to pray for one another in pairs or small groups. That attention to our personal well-being may free us to concentrate on the board business at hand. In fact, in taking time to deal with our immediate needs, we may be better able to conduct our business more effectively and efficiently. Our minds are more likely to be cleared of distractions, enabling us to articulate fresh ideas for the institution we are committed to serve.

Getting to know each other informally—before and after meetings and also at break times—can help us build a sense of commitment to one another. Being part of a board or committee should not preclude turning that body into a community—a place where at least certain needs can be discreetly shared. This should include not just needs of board members, but also needs of the staff and clients of the institution.

Lord, be present among us as we meet together to conduct business. Then may we minister to our sisters and brothers as whole persons, being sensitive to their needs and supporting them. At the same time, give us a renewed commitment and a clearer understanding of our task as members of this board. Amen.

— Lois Beck, Grantham, Pennsylvania

Listening Beneath

"Hear, O Israel: The Lord our God is one Lord; and you shall love the Lord your God with all your heart, and with all your soul, and with all your might."

— Deuteronomy 6:4, 5 (RSV)

"But I say to you that hear, Love your enemies, do good to those who hate you, bless those who curse you, pray for those who abuse you. And as you wish that men would do to you, do so to them."

— Luke 6:27, 28, 31 (RSV)

These two scriptures are called the Laws of Love. In them, Moses and Jesus both use the Hebrew word *shema*, which means to listen, contemplate, discern, and obey. The Latin meaning of obey is to listen beneath.

One chapter in Kent Ira Groff's excellent book, *Active Spirituality*, is entitled "Shema: The Language of Paying Attention." In it Groff urges us to pay attention to God and to each other. Sometimes in board meetings, because of time pressure or intensity or boredom, it is hard to stay focused. Yet it is important that we not only listen to each other, but that we *listen beneath* for the deeper meaning of what is being said.

In the movie "Dead Man Walking," Sister Helen Prejean ministers to a man on death row and to the families of the boy and girl who were murdered. What struck me was how intently she listened. I became impatient with her, wanting her to speak up and say, "Now listen here, you need to . . ." But I was listening to words while she was listening to souls. She was listening beneath.

"Attention is the only faculty of the soul which gives us access to God," said Simone Weil. It is also the only faculty with which we can genuinely hear each other; not just the words but the meaning of those words.

How often we see *shema* violated in our board rooms. An intense discussion is underway, but I have an important point I want to make. I'm not listening to what is being said; I'm formulating what I want to say. It is rude and violates *shema*. Listening beneath is hard work, but it is vital to our ministry.

In our drawing close to each other, help us to sense your closeness. As we seek to listen to each other, help us to discover with greater clarity your presence in our lives and our purpose in serving you. Amen.

We're far more likely to understand God when we understand each other.

— **Buck Blankenship, Charlotte, North Carolina**

What We Do—
What God Does

"Except the Lord build the house, they labor in vain that build it; except the Lord keep the city, the watchman waketh but in vain."

— Psalm 127:1 (KJV)

"Jesus said, 'Everyone then who hears these words of mine and acts on them will be like a wise man who built his house on rock. The rain fell, the floods came, and the winds blew and beat on that house, but it did not fall, because it had been founded on rock.'"

— Matthew 7:24, 25 (NRSV)

Efforts by believers include both what the believers do and what God does. God pays us what C.S. Lewis terms "the intolerable compliment" by making us partners with the God-Self. Whether it is an individual at work, or a company trying to work together, we are wise if we try to understand what we ought to do and what God will do.

What do we do? We meet and plan and set forth programs aimed at accomplishing something. We invite others to support what we are doing with prayers and gifts of time and money. We discuss and debate. We make, revise, discard plans, and substitute new ones. We hire and fire and evaluate staff. We hear reports of committees and move to accept, reject, amend, or refer back to committees. Having accepted a report, we try to find ways to implement it.

Someone observed that "committees keep minutes and waste hours." That is too severe. The genius of effective life and work is that we "do together," rather than trust the solo effort and judgment of any one person.

What does *God* do? The works of the Lord are "past finding out." God defined is God lost. Even so, it is possible to see what God is doing in what we do. To risk stating the obvious, God gives us life and breath to be about our tasks. God allows us to build on the work of those before us, and God promises that our work will be a legacy to those who come after us. God works when we sleep. God uses even our mistakes. God promises that what we undertake in God's name and for God's purpose in the world is undergirded by the Spirit "who works when and where and how he/she pleases."

We see what we do. We trust what God does, though we may not see it. We are partners with God.

"O Lord, support us all the day long of this troubled life, until the shadows lengthen, the evening comes, the busy world is hushed, the fever of life is over, and our work is done. Then, in your great mercy, grant us a safe lodging, a holy rest, and peace at the last, through Jesus Christ our Lord." Amen.
—**John Henry Cardinal Newman**

— **John David Burton, Williamsville, New York**

Fully Convinced
in the Face of Crisis

"Hoping against hope, [Abraham] believed that he would become 'the father of many nations,' according to what was said, 'So numerous shall your descendants be.' He did not weaken in faith when he considered his own body, which was already as good as dead (for he was about a hundred years old), or when he considered the barrenness of Sarah's womb. No distrust made him waver concerning the promise of God, but he grew strong in his faith as he gave glory to God, being fully convinced that God was able to do what he had promised."

— Romans 4:18-21 (NRSV)

T he morning dawned sunny, crisp, and clear. But my spirit felt partly cloudy. The church elder board would meet that evening to begin fitting together the pieces of a pastoral transition. Two of three pastors had resigned. Significant issues begged for attention. Various elders had differing opinions about what was needed. The future seemed daunting.

Boards sometimes face a crisis that calls for a clear vision. To have vision is to have faith. It is to be confident that God will be faithful even when the organization seems to be falling apart. God had promised that Abraham would be the father of many nations and that his descendants would be as numerous as the stars of the sky. God had promised, but things did not look promising. Abraham's body was "already as good as dead." Sarah's womb was barren. This was well before the days of fertility therapy. Still, Abraham was fully convinced that God was able to do what he had promised.

Abraham's story teaches us much about faith. First, faith does not deny the facts. Abraham faced the facts. He "considered his own body" and the "barrenness of Sarah." To have faith is not to deny reality. A board does not move toward its vision by denying current problems. Problems must be named before they can be resolved.

Second, faith remembers God's promises. Abraham clung to God's promises, believing that God would keep his word. In times of crisis, a board does well to recount the stories of how God called the organization into being and for what purpose. God never calls us where God will not lead us. Indeed, the most frequently recorded promise in the New Testament is that God's Spirit will be present with us to guide us.

Third, faith grows as we give glory to God. Abraham grew strong in his faith as he did just that. For Abraham this meant trusting God, "being fully convinced that God was able to do what he had promised." Boards should dream and discuss and make decisions. These are God-given abilities. But ultimately, boards must trust the well-being of the organization to the providential care of God.

God of Abraham and Sarah, grant us eyes of faith. May we face the facts before us. May we cling to your promises. May we entrust ourselves and our work to your care. Amen.

"Without faith, it is impossible to please God." —Hebrews 11:6 (NIV)

— J. Daryl Byler, Washington, D.C.

Restore Us, O God!

"Restore us, O God; let your face shine, that we may be saved."

— Psalm 80:3 (NRSV)

Not too efficient that day, I sat staring out of my office window at the rain, the mist, the gray. The dismal weather reflected my feelings. My desk had totally disappeared under an array of mailings and memos I could no longer keep in order. Important phone messages were going unanswered. New e-mails arrived, and the old ones were still unread. We had just learned that a colleague would be leaving, and we were stunned. I was due to go out of town in a few short days. With the dismal view outside reinforcing my inner gloom, where would I find the inspiration to tackle all that waited to be done?

Then something moving caught my attention. Down the sidewalk in the middle of the campus came a student riding a unicycle through the rain, in and out of puddles. Crazy, absurd, silly! The hilarity of that image altered my focus and lifted my spirits. It was as though God's face had suddenly shined into my gray day, reminding me not to take myself too seriously.

Restore us, O God;
    let your face shine,
    that we may be saved.
Restore us, O God
    – when our work overwhelms us
    – when relationships are broken
    – when we lose our way
    [add other phrases appropriate to the group]
Let your face shine
    – to comfort us in sorrow
    – to strengthen us when we are weary
    – to surprise us with joy
    [add phrases]
And may we be saved;
    for the kingdom, the power,
    and the glory are yours,
    now and forever.
                    Amen.

God's face is shining on us today, to restore us and save us. Amen.

— Sylvia Shirk Charles, Goshen, Indiana

Accepting Our "Flat Sides"

"Yes, the body has many parts, not just one part. If the foot says, 'I am not a part of the body because I am not a hand,' that does not make it any less a part of the body. But that is not the way God has made us. He has made many parts for our bodies and has put each part just where he wants it."

— I Corinthians 12:14, 15, 18, 21-26 (TLB)

Some years ago I participated with a group of managers in a test to help us understand ourselves better. The Myers-Briggs Personality Type Indicator places people into four categories according to personality tendencies. "Extroverts" are people who get energy from outside themselves; "introverts" from inside. "Sensing" people get information using their senses . . . "intuitive" types using their imaginations. "Thinking" types make decisions on logic, while "feeling" people make decisions on what is emotionally important to themselves and others. Finally, "judging" persons have a tendency to reach closure, to make decisions, in contrast to the "perceptive" types who want more information.

Psychological pigeon-holing can be a problem, but many work groups, including boards, use this technique to good advantage. If we understand our tendencies, and those of our colleagues, we can work together in a more powerful and harmonious way.

Our natural preference is to dwell on our strengths, but knowing our weaknesses, or our "flat sides," may be as important. When my strengths complement someone else's flat sides, and when my flat sides are surrounded by complementary strengths, then together we can function as a well rounded "person."

Organizations are made up of people with differing characteristics. Paul reminds us in I Corinthians 12 that the "weaker parts are indispensable." What are your flat sides? What are the flat sides of individuals on your board? If we can see our flat sides as indispensable, then we can organize for superior strength and results.

Grant us the courage and humility, dear God, to understand and accept our weaknesses in order to better serve you through the complementary strengths you provide in others. Amen.

When board members know and accept their weaknesses and strengths they experience *e pluribus unum*—out of many, one.

— **Lee Delp, Lansdale, Pennsylvania**

Truth-Telling

"Then we will no longer be like children, forever changing our minds about what we believe because someone has told us something different, or has cleverly lied to us and made the lie sound like the truth. Instead, we will lovingly follow the truth at all times—speaking truly, dealing truly, living truly— and so become more and more in every way like Christ who is the head of his body, the church. Under his direction the whole body is fitted together perfectly, and each part in its own special way helps the other parts, so that the whole body is healthy and growing and full of love."

— **Ephesians 4:14-16 (TLB)**

In the book *Why Am I Afraid To Tell You Who I Am?* (Tabor Publishing, 1969) John Powell, S.J. answers the question by quoting a close associate who said, "I am afraid to tell you who I am, because if I tell you who I am, you may not like who I am, and it's all that I have." Powell continues, "What you and I really need is a moment of truth and a habit of truth with ourselves. We have to ask ourselves in the quiet, personal privacy of our own minds and hearts, 'What games do I play?' 'What is it that I am trying to hide?' 'What is it that I hope to win?'"

Most boards need such a moment of truth. Where do the members of your board speak the truth? In the corridors? During a break? In the restroom? Over the phone before and after a meeting? It is only when we feel free to speak the truth as we see it, respecting the views of others, that we can fulfill our board responsibility to our members.

Outspoken members make themselves heard, but can the timid be heard? They, too, possess truth, though they may be reluctant to express it.

Ask yourselves at this meeting, is the conversation honest and open? Is the trust level strong enough that members feel free to risk expressing their true feelings and thoughts? During this meeting, check your ability to tell the truth. If you find the truth hard to express, maybe it is time to learn to trust, to take the risk that your opinion is important and needed to reach the best outcome.

Help each of us, loving God, to respect our fellow members. Help us to care enough to speak the truth. Help us to love enough to hear the truth. Amen.

Are we "tossed back and forth by the waves, and blown here and there by every wind," or have we grown up as a board so that we can "speak the truth with love"?

— Lee Delp, Lansdale, Pennsylvania

Just Plain
Hard Work

"Dear brothers [and sisters], honor the officers of your church who work hard and warn you against all that is wrong. Think highly of them and give them your whole-hearted love because they are straining to help you. And remember, no quarreling among yourselves. Dear brothers [and sisters] warn those who are lazy, comfort those who are frightened, take tender care of those who are weak, and be patient with everyone. See that no one pay back evil for evil, but always try to do good for each other and to everyone else. Always be joyful."

— I Thessalonians 5:12-15 (TLB)

Our son moved from our home in Pennsylvania to rural Kansas. He decided that two years of doing home repairs in voluntary service was the best use of his time before entering college. Rich was met with dirt, leaky sewers, and long hot days in the Kansas sun. His muscles were often sore. But as the days and months wore on, he began to hear the voice of God in the middle of just plain hard work. There were new friends, grateful "clients" who received help and gave love, and the retired Manitoba farmer-mentor who worked at his side, sharing the wisdom he gathered in the fields and barn. But it was in the endless hours of work that God spoke about life, the past, the future, and the direction he should go.

Much board work is like Rich's days in the Kansas sun— long, hard, tedious, and unglamourous. We need to make decisions without having all the facts, approve budgets which seldom provide for all that needs doing, contact donors, write min-utes, and, beyond all that, hear complaints. But often amid our hard work, in ways we don't always recognize, God speaks to us and shows us the way.

God, help us to be faithful in the tasks to which you have called us, regardless of how hard or tedious they may be. May we be conscious of your presence with us and may we be sensitive to your leading as we commit our work to you. Amen.

A man lamented to his rabbi: "I'm frustrated that my work leaves me with no time for study or prayer." The rabbi replied, "Perhaps your work is more pleasing to God than study or prayer."—Hasidic tale

— Lee Delp, Lansdale, Pennsylvania

Walking Rightly

"For we walk by faith, not by sight."

— II Corinthians 5:7 (NKJV)

" . . . walk worthy of the calling with which you were called."

— Ephesians 4:1 (NKJV)

"Trust in the Lord with all your heart, and lean not on your understanding; In all your ways acknowledge him and he will direct your paths."

— Proverbs 3:5-6 (NKJV)

Success, however we define it, can be dangerous. When we regard ourselves as successful, we have a tendency to start walking by sight instead of by faith; we deny that our total dependence is upon God.

Personally, and also corporately as organizations, God calls us to a life of faith, devoted in service to him. We are victorious (successful) when we walk by faith. Consider the message of I John 5:4 (RSV): "This is the victory that overcomes the world, even our faith."

Our temptation, to the contrary, is to maneuver ourselves and our organizations into such secure positions that faith is not necessary. Our subconscious goal is to be so secure that if God were to go out of business it would not affect our well-being, lifestyle, or retirement.

Walking rightly before God involves walking in faith and by faith. This is contrary to our natural tendency, which is to walk only where we can see to do only the things that make sense to us. God has better things in store for us if we walk rightly, by faith.

You are all-knowing and all-powerful. You love us with an everlasting love. You know better than we do what is best and what the future holds. Since faith, too, is a gift from you, give us the kind of faith that allows us to walk in a manner worthy of our calling. Teach us to walk as children of light. Amen.

God has better things in store for us if we walk rightly, by faith, and disregard who receives the credit.

— Christopher J. Doyle, Greenville, South Carolina

Taking
Every Thought Captive

"By the meekness and gentleness of Christ, I appeal to you—I, Paul, who am 'timid' when face to face with you but 'bold' when away! I beg you that when I come I may not have to be as bold as I expect to be toward some people who think that we live by the standards of this world. For though we live in the world, we do not wage war as the world does. The weapons we fight with are not the weapons of the world. On the contrary, they have divine power to demolish strongholds. We demolish arguments and every pretension that sets itself up against the knowledge of God, and we take captive every thought to make it obedient to Christ."

— II Corinthians 10:1-6 (NIV)

It is hard not to be swamped by all the information we receive and have available to us. In the workplace and in board meetings, we are bombarded with many things to read and digest. It is easy to get overloaded and switch off whatever is being discussed.

Our wandering minds may be easily diverted to dreaming of this year's vacation or moving into the many unsettled matters we harbor deep inside. However lively the discussion or disciplined the chairmanship, we may not always be able to concentrate on the issues at hand.

Whatever the temptation may be, disciplining our minds is the first step to overcoming that temptation. Every spiritual battle is a battle for supremacy of the mind. The apostle Paul suggests that this battle is won only by bringing our thoughts "captive" to Christ.

My computer illustrates what I mean. With a click of the mouse I can shrink the entire contents of the screen and "capture" them in a boxed area at the bottom. The result is an uncluttered screen, open and free to receive new information.

That is also what happens when I bring a thought captive to Christ. Suddenly it is put aside and my mind is clear to concentrate on the real issues. The distraction has passed. My mind is open to Christ, allowing him to work in my thoughts, words, and actions.

God, our minds are full. Conflicting thoughts jockey for attention—yesterday's highlights, tomorrow's dreams. Thoughts maneuver for priority. Cleanse the thoughts of our hearts by the inspiration of your Holy Spirit, that we may perfectly love you. Help us, we pray, to take hold of the divine powers and to use them to take captive every thought and make it obedient to you. Through Christ our Lord and Master, Amen.

"Create in me a new, clean heart, O God, filled with clean thoughts and right desires." —Psalm 51:10 (TLB)

— Trevor Durstin, London, England

Sensitivity to Others

"And there arose a sharp contention, so that they separated from each other."

— Acts 15:39 (RSV)

Mennonite Central Committee (MCC) had been in Europe with relief and service programs for more than 20 years. After being recipients, European Mennonites were gradually getting back on their feet following World War II and were beginning to contribute. Their young people worked alongside North American volunteers. It seemed like good cooperation.

That was just it—it "seemed" like cooperation—but it wasn't. The North Americans were in charge. The Europeans were permitted to contribute, but they had no voice in making decisions.

As MCC's Europe Director, I was determined to do something about this. My proposal called for the Dutch, German, French, and Swiss Mennonites to join with North Americans, represented by MCC, to establish a new organization. Each nationality would have one vote for each 10,000 church members. That meant the French and Swiss would each have one vote, the Germans would have two, the Dutch would have three. To protect against North American domination, I suggested that MCC have just one vote.

The day of the historic meeting came. All participating partners, including MCC, were represented. To satisfy the pietistic Swiss, French, and South German Mennonites, I began by stating the biblical basis for Christians engaging in "social services." A Dutch delegate led off by suggesting that a different passage of Scripture would be more appropriate. Not wanting to get hung up on what I thought was a minor point, I agreed.

Another Dutchman suggested a slight change in the introductory paragraph. Again, no problem. There was more discussion. Time went on, but we weren't getting anywhere. Should we or should we not join together in a new organization? The chairman was frustrated. I was confused.

Then it dawned on me. The Dutch had no intention of supporting the proposed plan. They were stalling, and time was running out. The meeting adjourned with the chairman offering a short prayer.

The lesson was clear. When you're a heavyweight, you're a problem for other people. MCC, with its comparatively massive resources, was once again seen as throwing its weight around. Though well intentioned, we were still telling them what to do and how to do it.

Within a year, the Europeans organized themselves into their own organization. Their message to MCC was: "See, we did it on our own. We have our own organization. Now let's cooperate."

Lord, when we are strong, when we want to be helpful, make us sensitive to the feelings of others. Spare us from throwing our weight around, unwittingly intimidating those who have fewer material resources. Grant us, we pray, a larger measure of humility. Amen.

— Peter J. Dyck, Scottdale, Pennsylvania

Call
to Unity

"Now I appeal to you, brothers and sisters, by the name of our Lord Jesus Christ, that all of you be in agreement and that there be no divisions among you, but that you be united in the same mind and the same purpose."

— I Corinthians 1:10 (NRSV)

The time was 1943; the place was Birmingham, England. Nine Quakers and one Mennonite were seated around the board table. We were opening more homes in the countryside for evacuees from the bombed and burning cities. With men drafted and women working in war industries, we were always short of personnel. The question before us now was how much we could compromise our standards to get the personnel we needed.

After a lengthy and animated discussion which threatened to polarize the group, the chair called for a period of silence. I had attended Friends (Quaker) meetings for worship and was intrigued with their long silences, but this was the first time I was experiencing silence as a problem-solving device in a board meeting. There was no need to instruct the participants on the value of silence. Quakers know that listening, not talking, is the key to every successful undertaking. First there is listening to each other, which Dietrich Bonhoeffer called "the first service that we can perform for anyone." And then there is listening to God. Quakers remember the statement of their founder George Fox, that "there is that of God in everyone." They are taught to listen to God's voice.

So there we sat, 10 adults, all looking at our full agenda and our watches. They knew from experience that "centering down" takes time. It took time to shut out the voices on the pros and cons of standards; it took time to become quiet and listen to the "still small voice" (I Kings 19:12).

It may have been five minutes, or perhaps it was 10 or more; I don't remember. All I recall is that when the chair finally asked a member to sum up what had been said (Quakers call it "discerning the sense of the meeting" [I Corinthians 12:28]), there was a totally different mood among us. There was peace and there was unity. I was amazed at the results—and the time we had saved.

Lord, help us in this meeting to be good listeners. Grant us the discipline to talk, but also to listen to what our brother and sister have to say. And above all, Lord, help us to listen to you. Amen.

— **Peter J. Dyck, Scottdale, Pennsylvania**

Remember
the Little Ones

"But Joseph said to them, 'Do not be afraid! Am I in the place of God? Even though you intended to do harm to me, God intended it for good, in order to preserve a numerous people, as he is doing today. So have no fear; I myself will provide for you and your little ones.'"

— Genesis 50:19-21 (NRSV)

Joseph was high in the bureaucracy of a very powerful nation, giving leadership to a huge famine relief ministry. He recognized his place under God's authority. He recognized that God was able to use the evil actions of his brothers for good. He forgave and cared for them.

It is intriguing that with all of the emotion of the moment, and with all the other things Joseph must have had on his mind, he remembered the "little ones."

God seems to have special concern for the "little ones" in the world—the children, the widows, the orphans. God lifts up for reward those who serve the "least of these." Organizations, in contrast, gravitate toward power and prestige. Big donors get the most attention and have the loudest voice in organizational policy. High-level staff have more access to decision-making than those who are lower down. Even organizations whose primary mission is to serve the disenfranchised and powerless sometimes fail to care well for the little ones who work in their offices, and they are often deaf to their voices.

It is whispered that an organization can function quite well if its president leaves town, but it would stop immediately if some of the less prestigious operational people stopped working. Everyone in the organization is important. Some of the most insightful and creative ideas come from the margins. The most important work of an organization is done by those who directly touch the persons the organization serves. Jesus and his love come alive in relationships more than in organizational policies or strategic plans.

A major responsibility of the board is to remember the little ones. This means establishing structures which give them voice and creating policies which care for them and treat them fairly.

Oh God, give us ears to hear the voices of the little ones in our world and in our organization. Give us loving hearts to care for them and creative minds to find ways to share power and strength. Amen.

Reflect on how each decision you make at this board meeting affects the "little ones" in your organization and the "little ones" you serve.

— John Eby, Dillsburg, Pennsylvania

Organizational Sanity

"Do not be conformed to this world, but be trans-
formed by the renewing of your minds, so that you
may discern what is the will of God—what is good
and acceptable and perfect. For by the grace given to
me I say to everyone among you not to think of your-
self more highly than you ought to think, but to think
with sober judgment, each according to the measure
of faith that God has assigned. For as in one body we
have many members, and not all the members have
the same function, so we, who are many, are one
body in Christ, and individually we are members one
of another. We have gifts that differ according to the
grace given to us . . ."

Romans 12:2-6a (NRSV)

J. B. Phillips paraphrases verse 3, "Don't cherish exaggerat-
ed ideas of yourself or your importance, but try to have a
sane estimate of your capabilities." Knowing who we are,
what gifts we have, and what niche we fill, and knowing how
the gifts God has given us complement the gifts God has given
others is the beginning of both personal and organizational
sanity.

A strong board has diversity. Different perspectives and mul-
tiple skills make a board more than the sum of its individual
members. To make that diversity work, each member must
know her/his capabilities and contribution. Pride and false mod-
esty inhibit the release of God's gifts. Group-think and unmiti-
gated conflict can destroy a board. Recognizing the unique gifts
of each member, and then carefully melding those strengths
together, creates an effective board.

Having a sane estimate and sober judgment of the capabilities of the organization is equally important. Many organizations fail completely or survive in mediocrity because they do not know themselves. Overestimating an organization's strength leads to taking on tasks that are beyond the organization's capabilities. Or it can result in casualness about potential risk and in complacency about relationships with supporters or customers. It is equally dangerous to underestimate capabilities. Opportunities for expanded ministry will be missed and creative innovations overlooked.

You, God, are father, son, and spirit. You created a world full of diversity. You give your church a rich variety of individuals and organizations. We celebrate that diversity and thank you for those unique gifts and missions. Release these gifts, we ask, and give us freedom and ability to share our perspectives and sensitivity to hear the perspectives of others. Inform our thoughts with your wisdom and guide our actions with your spirit. Give us sober judgment to know ourselves and clarity of vision to work together on the mission you have given us. Amen.

What are the unique gifts you bring to your board and the unique gift your organization brings to the world?

— John Eby, Dillsburg, Pennsylvania

Shrewdness for the Kingdom

"Then Jesus said to the disciples, 'There was a rich man who had a manager, and charges were brought to him that this man was squandering his property. So he summoned him and said to him, "What is this that I hear about you? Give me an accounting of your management, because you cannot be my manager any longer." Then the manager said to himself, "What will I do, now that my master is taking the position away from me? I am not strong enough to dig, and I am ashamed to beg. I have decided what to do so that, when I am dismissed as manager, people may welcome me into their homes." So, summoning his master's debtors one by one, he asked the first, "How much do you owe my master?" He answered, "A hundred jugs of olive oil." He said to him, "Take your bill, sit down quickly, and make it 50." Then he asked another, "And how much do you owe?" He replied, "A hundred containers of wheat." He said to him, "Take your bill and make it 80." And his master commended the dishonest manager because he had acted shrewdly; for the children of this age are more shrewd . . . than are the children of light.'"

— Luke 16:1-8 (NRSV)

The manager might have been incompetent, dishonest, lazy, or even burned out, but he wasn't stupid. He used his head rather than his body. He knew he needed friends and needed them quickly. So he devised a clever scheme. He altered the books! Their complicity in his clever scheme gave the benefactors added reason to treat him well.

By telling this story, Jesus was not condoning the manager's action, but he does seem to admire his cleverness. The manager knew how to make the system and structures of society work for him. That leads to the point of the story.

Jesus infers that those of us with Kingdom values must develop creativity, courage, analytic skill, and even shrewdness to understand the system so well that we can use it to accomplish Kingdom work. We are required to work within the constraints and ethics of fallen society, to design organizations, and to act in ways that translate good intentions into real-life practices. Our organizations do justice, care for needy persons, show love, empower people, and serve the common good. Incarnating Kingdom values in a competitive world may be the greatest challenge facing leaders who put the Kingdom first.

Creator and sustainer God, in our work of creating structures, setting strategies, choosing priorities, and forming policies, we commit ourselves to seek your Kingdom and not to be distracted by selfish ambition or limited by worldly concerns. We pray that you will give us wisdom, creativity, and understanding to translate Kingdom values into earthly actions. Amen.

How can you help God's Kingdom to come, God's will to be done, on earth as it is in heaven?

— John Eby, Dillsburg, Pennsylvania

Savoring
the Moments of our Days

"God has made everything suitable for its time; [and] has put a sense of past and future into [workers'] minds, yet they cannot find out what God has done from the beginning to the end. I know that there is nothing better for them than to be happy and enjoy themselves as long as they live; moreover, it is God's gift that all should eat and drink and take pleasure in all their toil. I know that whatever God does endures forever; nothing can be added to it, nor anything taken from it."

— Ecclesiastes 3:9, 11-14a (NRSV)

On a recent evening my daughter Sophia carried on an animated phone conversation with her friend Alyssa. One might wonder what toddlers find to talk about when they aren't playing together and can't see each other's faces. I found myself listening with amusement, but also with attentiveness.

Clearly her friend was asking Sophia what she was doing at that moment. I kept hearing the word "squares"; she and I had just finished mixing oatmeal, sugar, and butter for a pan of fruit squares. Then she began to describe the room—our kitchen—that she was in. "The walls?" I heard. "They're white. The door is white, too," she said. "Outside the window? It's dark."

This tone of conversation went on for some time—not straying from the topics of the room, bedtime, and what each would eat for a snack (at least as much as I could infer from one side of the conversation!). What a small world, I mused. Imagine an entire conversation about such minor details of life.

But then I thought again. Not only did the girls express keen interest in minute details of each other's surroundings, Sophia took great joy in it—as she does with so many "small" events of her life. A recently opened flower in our back garden. The taste of a plum, cold from the fridge—"like a freeze pop, Mom!" The never-failing routine of prayers before bed when we snuggle "just right," proceeding through a standard sequence of "thank-yous" to God. Most of my days, on the other hand, are future-oriented. As I wash tonight's dishes I think about what we'll eat for supper tomorrow, or plan next month's visit to friends in Ontario. My work days are filled with meetings or booking meetings—days, weeks, and months in advance. And my husband and I recently met with a financial advisor to discuss whether our retirement savings will cover our expenses.

What does this future thinking cost me? What does my daughter see in the "now" that I miss completely? "God had made everything suitable for its time," says the writer of Ecclesiastes. If it's only when I take that much-planned vacation, or when my daughter forces me to concentrate on bedtime prayers, that I truly experience the present, I will miss many of God's gifts.

God, help me to see that the future is in your hands. Give me joy in savoring the moments of my days, in really seeing all that is around me. For this day, give me pleasure in my toil and delight in your creation. Amen.

— **Deborah Fast, Akron, Pennsylvania**

Conflict and Hyperbole Among Colleagues

"Woe to you, scribes and Pharisees, hypocrites! For you lock people out of the kingdom of heaven. For you do not go in yourselves, and when others are going in, you stop them. You cross sea and land to make a single convert, and you make the new convert twice as much a child of hell as yourselves."

— Matthew 23:13-15 (NRSV)

A controversy erupted in 1997 among American evangelical publishers and biblical scholars about the New International Version (NIV), the most popular Bible ever printed. It revolved around the use of gender-inclusive language. An inclusive language version of the NIV had been published in Britain in 1995 and had been well received.

At issue was how much the biblical text should reflect language changes in a particular culture. For those who opposed changes, the issue centered on tampering with the text and changing the very words of God. Others insisted that the text ought to reflect changes that language itself undergoes in a society.

This was, it should be noted, an in-house fight. All participants were, in the words of one biblical scholar, "conservative evangelicals, totally committed to all the great evangelical doctrines of the historic faith—including the Bible as the authoritative, infallible, inspired, and completely truthful Word of God."

In Jesus' time, the party of the Pharisees was actually one of the renewal movements within Judaism. For them, observing

God's Law was a great privilege, and they sought to make it practical in their homes and communities, down to the smallest food laws. Later, some became believers in Jesus as Messiah and saw no conflict with continuing to observe the law. When Jerusalem and the temple were destroyed in 70 CE, the only party that survived in Palestine were the Pharisees, for their faith-practices were not centered in the temple, but in the homes of ordinary people.

Reading the Gospels, we naturally side with Jesus and his emphasis on the "weightier matters" of the law. But we must remember that this is only one side of the story. When we run into conflict, we tend to see our position as reasonable and logical and view all others in the worst possible light. Sometimes our stand on an issue may be more conservative, or it may pay more attention to details, or be less daring or risk-taking. In those times, we are good Pharisees! Our plan may be the one actually enabling an organization to survive. At other times, a more radical vision, like Jesus', should carry the day.

God, give us the wisdom to understand all sides of issues that confront us and the courage and discernment to make the right decisions. Help us to know when to be forthright and when to be cautious. Help us to remember that those with whom we may disagree most strongly are those who are at heart often most like us—indeed, bone of our bone and flesh of our flesh. Amen.

— **Reta Halteman Finger, Harrisonburg, Virginia**

The Trapeze Artist—
A Parable

"To everything there is a season, and a time for every purpose under the heaven; a time to be born, and a time to die; a time to plant, and a time to pluck what is planted; a time to kill and a time to heal; a time to break down, and a time to build up."

.— Ecclesiastes 3:1-3 (NKJV)

The children watch breathlessly. The arena is still. The only movement is that of the trapeze artists as they swing high above the anxious crowd. Then one performer lets go of the swing, leaps into the air, does a double somersault and, with perfect timing and precision, grasps the outstretched hands of her aerial partner. The crowd sighs. Their daring act successfully completed, both performers take a graceful dive into the net. The appreciative audience applauds.

This circus scene shows at least three things to persons in the flurry of organizational life.

One, the time comes when we must make a conscious decision to let go. It may be a treasured idea, but we must let it go to make room for a new one. It might mean letting go of a position which has meant much to us—to make room for fresh leadership. It may require letting go of a demanding schedule—to catch a needed breath and some therapeutic change. In our personal lives, it may mean releasing loved ones—so they can find their own identities.

Two, the trapeze artists teach us about risk-taking. Do you know any worthwhile venture that does not involve risk? Risk is an essential part of life. Casey Stengel, former New York

Yankees manager, asked his players, "Did you ever see a guy steal second base with his foot tied to first?" Or from the world of healing, can surgery be performed without risk, on the part of the patient and the surgeon?

Three, we may ask, but what about the safety net? No doubt about it, it's there for us, too. And we do need it. Do organizational performers have a safety net? Most definitely. In the words of Jesus, "Where two or three are gathered in my name, there am I in their midst."

Lord of Life, be with us in the crucial times of our lives. Make us conscious of your presence in the still, as well as in the troubled, waters. Amen.

Wisdom comes in knowing when to let go. Courage is in the release.

— Gilbert E. Fleer, Columbia, Missouri

Weep with
the Weeping

"Let love be genuine; hate what is evil, hold fast to what is good . . . be patient in suffering, persevere in prayer . . . Rejoice with those who rejoice, weep with those who weep."

— Romans 12:9, 12b, 15 (NRSV)

A child came home from school and told her mother that her friend had been pushed into a mud puddle by a bully. Her mother asked her what she had done. "Did you help her out of the mud puddle?" "No," replied the daughter, adding that her friend was so upset she refused to be moved. "Did you go for help?" asked the mother. "No," replied the daughter, "I couldn't leave her there by herself." "Then what did you do?" asked the mother. "I sat down in the puddle," replied the daughter, "and I cried with her."

That story describes how I felt about arriving in Lebanon in April 1996, the same day Israel bombed a UN base sheltering refugees, killing more than 100 civilians. A long-term local Mennonite Central Committee employee, Bassam, described his feelings of hopelessness. I listened helplessly as Bassam expressed his frustration in trying to comfort his two young daughters who watched on TV as their town was being shelled. His family had earlier been displaced by the fighting in the South. He was weary after a week of intensive bombardment, to say nothing of living for years with instability and constant danger. In addition, he was busy filling in gaps left by other Lebanese relief agencies.

I asked Bassam if he had any hopes for the situation to end soon. His response sobered me even further. "Our problem with hopes is that we had hopes several years ago for a negotiated settlement. Since then there have been many difficulties with the process. There have been many attacks since the last agreement. Sometimes we feel tired. Now we are completely tired. We cannot imagine what the future will be."

I was saddened by his lack of hope and groped for words which would not sound cheap to someone in his situation. I cared deeply, but the situation was beyond my ability to comprehend. I put together several words to that effect. His response was, "We need your prayers. You are people of good hearts, and we know that you will respond." I gave this friend, a Muslim brother, my pledge that North American Christians would pray for him and the people of Lebanon.

Listening God, from the beginning of the history of humankind you have heard and responded to the cries of people in distress. Give us your heart for those who suffer. Teach us the wisdom of waiting with them in their pain. Give us the courage to experience their weeping so that we will truly know how to be with them. Through Jesus Christ our gracious Lord, Amen.

— **Ardith Frey, Winnipeg, Manitoba**

No Limos, Please

"Then Jesus, when he had found a young donkey, sat on it; as it is written, 'Fear not, daughter of Zion; behold, your King is coming, sitting on a donkey's colt.'"

—John 12:14 (NKJV)

We've all seen them—sleek, long, luxurious limousines at airports and high-priced hotels. Interiors that look like small lounges, outfitted with telephone, reading lights, and a not-so-hidden bar. Though appearing to be nearly a block long, they seldom have more than two passengers and a driver with tinted glasses. The exteriors have elegant little lights. Now those make sense! Like eighteen-wheelers, limousines need lots of light to keep other vehicles from running into them.

Millard and I were six years into marriage. Due largely to Millard's keen business skills, we had literally gone from rags to riches. However, material wealth did not bring us a storybook marriage or happiness. We came close to divorce. Out of that crisis, God called us to give our money and possessions to charity and to find our place in full-time Christian service. The result was founding Habitat for Humanity International. Since scaling down our lifestyle, limousines and similar luxuries have a hollow ring with us.

When I see limousines or expensive houses occupied by one or two people or a diamond-studded item in a catalog, I translate that into how many families could be helped to own their own homes with that excess.

My ideal is Mother Teresa who, when she was given a limousine to get around in Calcutta, sold it and built a shelter for homeless lepers.

The only vehicle Jesus of Nazareth used was a young donkey. If he were living in these times, I think he would say, "No limousines, please."

Lord Jesus, we know you got around by walking and riding an occasional donkey. Help us keep this in mind when responsibilities call us to distant places. Forgive us when we spend a lot of extra money on ourselves. Help us to remember your warning not to lay up treasures for ourselves. Rather, let our desire be to seek first your Kingdom and all its richness. Only then will we truly be rich in your sight. Amen.

"There are no great things; only small acts done with great love." —Mother Teresa

— Linda Caldwell Fuller, Americus, Georgia

A Mind
Focused on God

"Blessed is the man who walks not in the counsel of the ungodly, nor stands in the path of sinners, nor sits in the seat of the scornful; But his delight is in the law of the Lord, and in his law he meditates day and night. And he shall be like a tree planted by the rivers of water, that brings forth its fruit in its season, whose leaf also shall not wither; And whatever he does, shall prosper."

— Psalm 1:1-3 (NKJV)

In preparing for a weekend retreat I came across the writings of Frank Laubach. Dr. Laubach was the famous literacy expert who coined the slogan, "Each one teach one." In his missionary work, Dr. Laubach lived alone in a remote area of the Philippines, among people who were not receptive to the Christian gospel. During that time he made a concerted effort to think about God all the time. He admitted that it was very difficult to do, but he found that the struggle brought a sense of inner peace and a clarity of thought, even about things mundane.

More recently I learned about focusing on God from a special little boy, our grandson Benjamin. Our son Chris is a campus pastor in Savannah, Georgia. One day he was driving to a shopping mall with four-year-old Benjamin. They were chatting away about various things when Ben fell silent. Chris kept talking but got no response. He became a bit more insistent, wanting some answers to his questions. Ben, somewhat irritated, replied, "Be quiet, Daddy. I'm thinking about God!"

Lord, help us to be still and know that you are God. Give us such a strong sense of your presence that we will be conscious of you even while thinking and talking about the business of this meeting. [Silence.] Amen.

Things fall into place when God is at the top of our thoughts.

— Millard Fuller, Americus, Georgia

Serving Through Leadership

"Serve wholeheartedly, as if you were serving the Lord, not men [and women], because you know that the Lord will reward everyone for whatever good he [or she] does, whether . . . slave or free."

— Ephesians 6:7, 8 (NIV)

S̲ome years ago I was asked to speak on "Serving Through Leadership." My first thought was that while there are many aspects of leadership, the first is service. An attitude of serving always enhances leadership.

In looking for an illustration, I remembered a story about a church who managed to pay their bills but didn't seem to have money to do the things the church really could and should have been doing. As is sometimes the case, everyone was looking to fix blame. An older member blurted out to the minister one day, "Preacher, if you would just preach sermons that would get people's hearts right, then they would give enough money to the church." The minister countered with, "It is true that if peoples' hearts were right they would give more to the church. However, if people would start turning loose more of their money and investing something in this church, it would go a long way toward getting their hearts right."

The minister was right. When you invest something of yourself in an organization, the organization becomes much more important to you. You begin to care about how the organization spends its money and if it has money to meet its obligations. You begin to care about the organization's policies, since they reflect on you. The great Russian author Solzhenitsyn observed that when he was in prison, he could quickly tell who would survive. Those who survived were the ones who were willing to help others.

Tom Peters, in his book *In Search of Excellence,* makes the point that companies are successful because of the "X factor." It's the oomph, the pizzazz, the something extra. So whether teaching, coaching, preaching, volunteering, running for public office, or even doing the mundane chores of the day, remember to give a little extra. The extra is truly serving through leadership.

Gracious God, fill our hearts with your love so that we may willingly serve others in your name. Amen.

— **Sandra Graham, Greenville, South Carolina**

Thumbs Up

*"May the Lord show mercy to the household of
Onesiphorus, because he often refreshed me and was
not ashamed of my chains. On the contrary, when he
was in Rome, he searched hard for me until he found
me."*

— II Timothy 1:16-17 (NIV)

A few years ago, drawn by a vision of the future, I felt
called to introduce major changes in our organization. A
woman, likely to experience a major impact by the antic-
ipated changes, appeared in my office doorway. I was glad I was
on the phone, for I was sure she came either to express her disapproval or to request special consideration. I was not prepared
for what she did. Instead of a scowl, her face broke into a smile
and she gave me a "thumbs up." I wonder what she would have
said, had I not been on the phone. I was so taken up with what
I expected her reaction to be that I almost failed to receive the
blessing of her affirmation.

Leadership often brings us to lonely places where we long for
refreshment and blessing. Sometimes this happens in unexpected ways. Attending the worldwide conference of my church
denomination in Calcutta was, for those of us from the West,
an enriching experience. While the churches in the West have
enormous resources and sophisticated programs, we were
moved by the spontaneous joy and spiritual vitality of the
churches in the South.

Paul was alone and deserted, often in Roman prisons which
were known to sap vitality and bring gloom to the spirit.
Imagine him, surrounded by the hostile might of Rome, pon-
dering his lot night and day. Suddenly his dear friend

Onesiphorus appears. We know little about Onesiphorus. He was apparently not a person of great status or influence. Yet Paul prays divine mercy upon him out of gratitude for how he "often refreshed" Paul spiritually and physically. Onesiphorus revived Paul's flagging spirit, or, as Moffat's translation puts it, "he braced me up." Onesiphorus was not ashamed or afraid to be identified with Paul, a prisoner, but searched him out and ministered to him.

Thank you Lord for those who buoy us up when the going is tough. Open our hearts to your blessings. Make us ready to receive your care, especially from those from whom we least expect it. Surprise us with your love. Amen.

— **Stanley W. Green, Elkhart, Indiana**

Courage and Faithfulness to Pursue a Vision

"My brothers and sisters, whenever you face trials of any kind, consider it nothing but joy, because you know that the testing of your faith produces endurance; and let endurance have its full effect, so that you may be mature and complete, lacking in nothing. If any of you is lacking in wisdom, ask God, who gives to all generously and ungrudgingly, and it will be given you. But ask in faith, never doubting, for the one who doubts is like a wave of the sea, driven and tossed by the wind."

— James 1:2-6 (NRSV)

I was presented with a daunting task on the eve of Atlanta's preparations for the Summer Olympic Games. At the very visible northern entrance stood an abandoned hotel. Such a hulking eyesore could not be tolerated. Our plan, as a nonprofit developer of affordable housing, was to renovate it, with 25% of the units reserved for the formerly homeless. The $9.5 million cost was steep, the construction challenges of renovating a deteriorated structure were numerous, and the approvals we needed seemed endless. The outcome was uncertain. Through perseverance our vision became a beautiful reality. The former eyesore is now home for 120 individuals.

Nehemiah was an Old Testament prophet with faith and courage. God called him to rebuild the walls of Jerusalem. We know the story. Not to be forgotten are the obstacles he and his followers had to surmount. Nehemiah warned his people of the hardhearted opposition to their work. Chapter four records that

" . . . half of my servants worked on construction, and half held the spears, shields, bows, and body-armor. . ."

The New Testament is replete with examples of courage in pursuit of worthy vision. Jesus' familiar command to "take up the cross and follow me" is not an exhortation to bear any burden or pain, but rather an invitation to walk willingly in his service. To do so requires courage, but also offers for a reward a journey of joyful self-discovery, as James' letter assures us.

Directors are called to address monumental social problems and challenges. Fomidable risks and barriers, uncertainties and questions stand in the way of achieving our vision. These occasions demand courage and faithfulness.

Lord, being placed before our present-day "walls of Jericho" is both a privilege and a responsibility. Grant us courage and faithfulness to pursue your plans for us, knowing that our pursuit will not be in vain. Amen.

— **Bruce Gunter, Atlanta, Georgia**

Consider
the Apricot Tree

"Satisfy us in the morning with your steadfast love, so that we may rejoice and be glad all our days. Make us glad as many days as you have afflicted us, and as many years as we have seen evil. Let your work be manifest to your servants, and your glorious power to their children. Let the favor of the Lord our God be upon us, and prosper for us the work of our hands— O prosper the work of our hands!"

— Psalm 90:14-17 (NRSV)

Nature is full of projects that fail. At least it seems that way. Somehow what seems like failure is especially evident in the spring. For example, behind our house a small apricot tree grows. Every spring it begins to bloom—delicate, pinkish white blossoms appear just as we are getting so tired of winter that it seems it will never be over. We watch the tree's gently changing loveliness—and hold our breaths. For, almost every year, it starts to bloom just a little too soon, and a frost destroys its flowers and prevents any possibility of getting any apricots from the tree.

Across the lane at the bluebird house, bluebirds have appeared the last few years, eager and ready to work. In a painstakingly slow process, they flit toward the birdhouse, carrying the materials for a nest into the box. Last year they actually laid their eggs and hatched them, but then the weather turned hot and dry for so long that the baby birds could not survive. This year, after building a neat nest, they were chased away by their tree swallow neighbors.

Despite these apparent failures, we know that the apricot tree will bloom again next year and that the bluebirds will make another nest. It's just instinct, we say.

What does that have to do with us? I suggest instead that they are being true to God's creative purpose for them. Each day they do the work for that day. While they are always directed toward the goal, they are never defined by it alone. For those of us working for organizations who seek to faithfully respond to the broad spectrum of human need, it may be helpful to claim rather than dismiss the experience of the apricot tree and the bluebirds. We have a sense of where we are headed and the "product" we would like to see. Yet we need not measure our work solely by the end result, but equally by the faithfulness with which we carry out each step.

Loving and creative God, you have called us to our tasks as people created in your image. We want you to make our work fruitful. Make us aware of how we go about that work, so that the process of our meetings and deliberations has its own beauty and value. Amen.

"A landscape can sing about God." —Dag Hammarskjöld

— Nancy R. Heisey, Harrisonburg, Virginia

Stumbling Toward Diversity

"On Peter's arrival Cornelius met him, and falling at his feet, worshiped him. But Peter made him get up, saying, 'Stand up; I am only a mortal.' And as he talked with him, he went in and found that many had assembled; and he said to them, 'You yourselves know that it is unlawful for a Jew to associate with or to visit a Gentile; but God has shown me that I should not call anyone profane or unclean. So when I was sent for, I came without objection. Now may I ask why you sent for me?'"

— Acts 10:25-29 (NRSV)

Recently Patricia, a friend from Malaysia, was traveling from Philadelphia to a meeting in New Orleans. Knowing that her resources were limited, I packed a small bag of snacks for her in case she decided to save money at the meeting by skipping meals. After her return, she told me that she was offended by my gift, suspecting that it implied that I thought of her as poor and in need of help. Her response hurt me, but our friendship was important enough to both of us that we kept talking.

This reminded me of an early experience I had when I was the only woman at a meeting I needed to attend for my job. While keeping up with the agenda and speaking on matters that concerned me were not hard for me, I found facing mealtimes and post-meeting discussions about whether to go swimming or to a movie to be intimidating and frightening. Larry, also attending, seemed aware of my discomfort. On several occasions he made a specific point of including me in coffeebreak circles. I was tempted to interpret his interest as patronizing. Over years of working with him as a colleague, however, I learned more about his respect for and openness to people who are different from him.

Experiences with both Patricia and Larry taught me something about what it takes to allow diversity to shape our work. What I've learned reminds me of the story of Peter and Cornelius. Both Peter and Cornelius, when they faced the reality of the barriers which separated them as Jew and Gentile, got it wrong at first. But because both of them were willing to listen to and obey God's voice, they were able to take the next step—to ask questions which kept the door open through the wall that separated them.

God of the many people who make up this wide world, guide our efforts to truly represent the beautiful diversity of your family in our organization. Forgive us when we don't care enough to include different voices around our board table. Make us humble when we try to be inclusive and fail. Keep us free of long-held resentments, and help us step-by-step to allow all of us to offer our gifts to your work. Amen.

"Christ enough to break all barriers." —John Gardener, a South African schoolteacher

— Nancy R. Heisey, Harrisonburg, Virginia

Holy Resting

"But those who wait for the Lord shall renew their strength, they shall mount up with wings like eagles, they shall run and not be weary, they shall walk and not faint."

— Isaiah 40:31 (NRSV)

"The apostles gathered around Jesus, and told him all that they had done and taught. He said to them, 'Come away to a deserted place all by yourselves and rest a while.'"

— Mark 6:30-31 (NRSV)

"But now more than ever the word about Jesus spread abroad; many crowds would gather to hear him and to be cured of their diseases. But he would withdraw to deserted places and pray."

— Luke 5:15-16 (NRSV)

If we contemplate a candle long enough, we will discover several themes. We will be reminded of the ebb of our lives. It tells us that the day is slipping by. It invites us to look into the dark spots of our souls and bring light there. It teaches us not to burn the candle at both ends. Implicit here is a mandate from scripture: the call to come apart and rest awhile.

Not lazy or indulgent, holy resting deepens the quality of our living. We are trained to be doers, not dreamers; makers, not seers. But this call confronts us to pause and uncover the pockets of spiritual fatigue within us.

Rest is just as holy as work. There is a story told about Abbot Anthony, one of the desert fathers. A hunter who came upon him and the brothers relaxing and resting in the wilderness expressed his disapproval. Abbot Anthony told him to put an arrow in his bow and shoot it, which he did. Then the abbot told him to shoot another—and another and another. The hunter protested that if he bent his bow all the time, it would break. "So it is also in the work of God. If we push ourselves beyond measure, the brethren will collapse. It is right, therefore, from time to time, to relax their efforts," was the Abbot's reply.

Between meetings and conference calls, we can practice the posture of waiting. When we sit in this way, we are relaxing the bow; we are allowing ourselves to be cradled in the sighing mystery of Christ praying for us. This is one way to avoid a spiritual white-out, to keep the candle burning that lights our souls.

Empty us, O God
  of aching weariness,
  waning commitment,
  and fading vision.
Gentle us into quiet and uncurling fingers,
  letting go of heavy expectations
  and paralyzing fears.
Sustain us in this deliberation
  and give us Divine Perspective
  that we may be softened by the light
That invites holy resting. Amen.

No matter how valuable our work, the empty vessel must be filled.

— Linda Helmus, Lancaster, Pennsylvania

New Members
of the Body

"I therefore, the prisoner in the Lord, beg you to lead a life worthy of the calling to which you have been called, with all humility and gentleness, with patience, bearing with one another in love, making every effort to maintain the unity of the spirit in the bond of peace. There is one body and one Spirit . . . But each of us was given grace according to the measure of Christ's gift . . .The gifts he gave were that some would be apostles, some prophets, some evangelists, some pastors and teachers, to equip the saints for the work of ministry, for building up the body of Christ, . . .But speaking the truth in love, we must grow up in every way unto him who is the head, into Christ."

— Ephesians 4:1-4a, 7, 11, 12, 15 (NRSV)

Today we welcome new members into this ever-changing body. St. Paul teaches us that every member of Christ's body is important because Christ has given him or her a gift that is essential for the whole body to grow to maturity. Paul reminds us that humility, gentleness, and bearing with each other in love are the way those gifts are drawn together in the unity of the Spirit.

Christian boards feel the same pressure we feel in our work at home—to work fast and smart, to make a good impression on our peers, and to make no mistakes. We hold St. Paul's image of the body of Christ in tension with this business model. Let us take time in these meetings to acknowledge the weariness we have brought with us. Let us take time to minister to each other, to learn the joys and sorrows that each one is feeling.

We acknowledge the special pressures new members feel, struggling to make sense of the mountain of paper distributed before and during the meeting. Let old-timers be careful in using acronyms and other insider language. Let them take seriously the responsibility to be good mentors to new members. Let new members call for explanations so that they can boldly share the gifts that Christ has given each of them for building up the body of Christ.

Gracious God, we come to you in the name of Jesus our Lord, praying for your Spirit to move in our midst. [If available, sing or read slowly the hymn, "Gracious spirit, dwell with me."] "Now to him who by the power at work within us is able to accomplish abundantly far more than we can ask or imagine, to him be glory in the church and in Christ Jesus to all generations, forever and ever." Amen. — **Ephesians 3:20-21 (NRSV)**

Through the power of the Spirit, God can do more through us in these meetings than we can presently ask or imagine.

— Anna Juhnke, North Newton, Kansas

Decisions
Under Pressure

"But Jesus bent down and started to write on the ground with his finger. When they kept on questioning him, he straightened up and said to them, 'If any one of you is without sin, let him be the first to throw a stone at her.' Again he stooped down and wrote on the ground."

— John 8:6b-8 (NIV)

Many decisions are hard to make, and some are made harder by time pressures. This pressure, it seems, is increased by technology. The capacity to fax, e-mail, make conference calls, and reach persons on their cell phones leads us to believe that we can make instant decisions. Persons affected by our decisions are often either virtual or real participants in this process by their electronic access. No longer are decisions made in the isolation of back rooms or board rooms. Increasingly persons expect to influence decisions directly, or to be promptly notified about them, complete with full explanations. How can the 21st century Christian decision-maker deal wisely with these pressures?

One of my favorite Bible stories speaks to this issue. When the Pharisees confronted Jesus about the adulterous woman, the pressure was on him to come up with an instant response. He clearly wanted to support Jewish law. He also wanted to show mercy to the woman. To create a momentary delay, he stirred in the dirt with his finger. He bought some time, maybe to think, maybe to create anticipation, maybe to show respect for all parties. But he delayed for a moment.

The lesson for today? Some of our decisions may need to be delayed. We must not be pressured to make decisions prematurely by the intrusion or confrontation of technological wonders. Delays are not always a sign of weakness or indecision. Sometimes they are a sign of wisdom and compassion.

Dear God, we live in a world that is in a hurry for everything, including decisions. It is also a world that is increasingly quarrelsome and full of conflict. You have called us to be decision-makers. Sometimes when faced with our most difficult decisions, we would rather run and hide, or have you appoint someone else in our place. But we know we cannot, and that you have called us to stand in your place as fairminded adjudicators of order. Thank you for the example of your son Jesus who taught us to be deliberate in our search for the right answer. Amen.

Pausing as Jesus did can help us to be better decision-makers.

— Gerald Kaufman, Akron, Pennsylvania

Making
the Tough Decisions

"As you know and as God is our witness, we never came with words of flattery or with a pretext for greed; nor did we seek praise from mortals, whether from you or from others, though we might have made demands as apostles of Christ. But we were gentle among you, like a nurse tenderly caring for her own children. So deeply do we care for you that we are determined to share with you not only the gospel of God but also our own selves, because you have become very dear to us. As you know, we dealt with each one of you like a father with his children, urging and encouraging you and pleading that you lead a life worthy of God, who calls you into his own kingdom and glory."

— I Thessalonians 2:5-8, 11, 12 (NRSV)

Early in my role as a board executive I was confronted with some tough personnel decisions, which were especially sensitive because of race and gender. My natural inclination is to avoid conflict and smooth over disagreements. To risk change is never easy, especially when people and families are involved. How do a board and its leaders, committed to the lifestyle of Jesus, make the tough call?

In the scripture from Thessalonians Paul offers two images of his relationship with the church—a nurse (v. 7) and a father (v. 11). The nurse brings gentleness and care. The father offers direction. Both kinds of action are needed. Men and women alike can do both.

Healthy boards use both styles and include the perspectives of people who represent these different qualities in decision-making. In the case I described, we attempted to be gentle, even though we did not back away from necessary change. Wisdom, mingled with tears and pain, enabled a decision that proved over time to be right.

Tough decisions require gentleness combined with willingness to act on behalf of the common good. God modeled this capability in sacrificing Jesus for the salvation of the world. Can we today be both nurses and courageous leaders in the decisions facing us?

In the business facing this board today, we pray for the graces of the Spirit so that we act with love and concern for the well-being of others. We also ask for clarity of direction and courage to act when our opinions differ and the well-being of people is at stake. Forgive us for floundering at times out of fear or cowardice. Forgive us also for being impetuous when we become impatient. Give us wisdom to know when we face either of these temptations. We commit ourselves and our agenda to you, praying that your agenda for us may increasingly be the preoccupation of our lives. Through Jesus Christ, our example and Savior. Amen.

When we sincerely act out of concern for God's purposes in the world, God will honor and bless our decisions.

— James M. Lapp, Sellersville, Pennsylvania

When the Budget Falls Short

"I have learned to be content with whatever I have. I know what it is to have little, and I know what it is to have plenty. In any and all circumstances I have learned the secret of being well fed and of going hungry, of having plenty and of being in need. I can do all things through him who strengthens me . . . And my God will fully satisfy every need of yours according to his riches in glory in Christ Jesus. To our God and Father be glory forever and ever. Amen."

— Philippians 4:11b-13, 19, 20 (NRSV)

Being short of money is never easy. It seems even worse when a board or corporate structure finds itself in arrears. We blame, we whine, we become anxious or discouraged. Before we know it, morale sags and we lose hope.

Philippians 4 speaks about the apostle Paul's attitude regarding money. While the issues are more complex for an organization than for an individual, I suggest the attitudes Paul expressed are appropriate for board members. Contentment, trust, and confidence in God's ability to meet our needs provide perspective for all situations in life.

If our mission is of God, and if our decisions are shaped by the Spirit of God, we dare trust that this same God will provide the resources to meet the material needs of our organization. Prayer is not a substitute for careful planning and responsible leadership. Neither should prayer be an after-thought when all else fails. Seeking divine guidance and depending on divine resources is the formula for hope and joy, even when we live with financial uncertainties.

Confidence in God's riches in Christ Jesus can revive our morale, expand our horizons, renew our commitment to the task, and lead us to offer doxologies of praise: "To our God and Father be glory forever and ever." *Amen.*

We confess, O God, our tendencies to act self-sufficiently and then to worry when things seem out of control. We are especially prone to take things into our own hands when the budget is tight or in the red. Forgive us for our lack of faith and our failure to trust in your boundless resources. Again this day, we acknowledge it is your work in which we are engaged. We want to be dependent on you even though we find dependence a difficult challenge. Guide our deliberations so that they are infused with hope, contentment, and joy, and truly become a doxology of praise to you. Amen.

Our feelings about money are a good barometer of our true priorities, "for where your treasure is, there will your heart be also." — Matthew 6:21

— James M. Lapp, Sellersville, Pennsylvania

Small Sleeping Bags and Big Alarm Clocks

"Watch out! Don't let my sudden coming catch you unaware; don't let me find you living in careless ease, carousing and drinking and occupied with the problems of this life, like all the rest of the world. Keep a constant watch. And pray that if possible you may arrive in my presence without having to experience these horrors."

— Luke 21:34-38 (TLB)

Competence, like indifference, can be a dangerous thing. Leaders may lapse into the drowsiness of over-confidence. We sleepwalk through our tasks, we know them so well. Eventually we no longer see things we used to see; we cease to hear cues we used to pick up so deftly. This powerful, narcotic routine dulls creative faith and awareness of God's life-giving Spirit.

While traveling through California I picked up a copy of *The Los Angeles Times* which reported on Yukon Quest, a 1,000 mile dog-sled race from Yukon to Fairbanks. Life on the trail was pictured as lyrical and powerfully alive. The harsh, pristine wilderness heightened the senses of the mushers, as it quickened the pulses of the dogs. Each moment held both indescribable beauty and lethal danger. Every turn in the trail could expand the soul or snuff out life. Driving this knife edge offered the sensation of being fully awake, each fiber of body and spirit infused with that divine elixir called life.

A musher's greatest fear, it was said, is oversleeping. They do not want to be overtaken. The best mushers are reportedly known by their small sleeping bags and big alarm clocks. What a potent image! It gathers up vividly what Jesus asks for from his followers. He knows our impulse to lose ourselves in some downy, warm place. To become supremely comfortable in a proven role. To shut out the signs that challenge or warn. To abandon ourselves unreservedly to our comfort zone. To put off the further steps of real faith.

But as the mushers know well, this is not real life. There are no breathtaking vistas in the sleeping bag. Life is in the bark of the dogs, the spray of snow from the runners, the brilliant sunshine drenching a valley in winter. That is why we Christians were first known as Followers of the Way. That is where real life awaits the disciple.

Preserve us, O God, from the drowsiness of competence and complacency. Where we have settled into those warm, downy places of conscience, of exercising our routines, of safe leadership, of self-interest, of familiar relationships, rouse us to full wakefulness . . .

>   *that we not sleepwalk through our tasks . . .*
>   *that we not miss the stirring of your Spirit . . .*
>   *that we draw on the full strength of your presence . . .*
>   *that we be brought safely to our destination.*
>   *In Christ's name we pray, Amen.*

Small sleeping bags and big alarm clocks: a recipe for real, faithfull living.

— Jonathan P. Larson, Atlanta, Georgia

Glistening Oil
on a Bald Pate

"The wind blows where it chooses, and you hear the sound of it, but you do not know where it comes from or where it goes. So it is with everyone who is born of the Spirit."

— John 3:8 (NRSV)

One of my most humbling lessons is that the real Holy Spirit action, the appearance of authentic signs of the new creation, often happens on the way toward my big intentions or objectives. The Kingdom winks out to me most compellingly from these small and uncrafted events of life.

I had a much needed reminder of this recently when our adult daughter, reflecting on our Sunday together, said that the most powerful spiritual moment for her came when "Mac" McDonald, a strapping African American member of our congregation, knelt to be anointed with oil. His shaved head glistened with the sheen of the oil as it ran down his head and onto his collar and shirt. The numinous moment carried out to at least one person in the congregation the very nearness of the Kingdom. It spoke wordlessly about the goodness and beauty of God's Spirit. It whispered something about the comfort and peace, about a touch of the sacred, that the new creation bears into our otherwise arid lives.

But my focus as pastor, of course, had been on the prayers, the songs and hymns, the texts we had researched, the deftly chosen illustrations. The Spirit found an opening somewhere else. Left a divine signature without my knowing collaboration. Side-stepped my careful plan. And there it shone more winsomely than it ever has through my sermons or stories—from the glistening pate of my brother Mac.

This beguiles me. Humbles me. Intrigues me. For I am once again reminded of this stirring in the world that surpasses my purpose or my genius; surpasses my humanly impressive, but flawed, vision; surpasses my very sharpest skills. This, indeed, inspires me to awe, to wonder, and to watch. From what common gesture, from behind what mundane detail of the day, will this rare radiance appear when I least expect it and announce that God is near? Without this I cannot really live. Without this my most brilliant inspirations are stillborn. Without this the sails hang limp and my vessel is becalmed far from harbor.

O God, help me to recognize and rejoice in the glistening of your presence even apart from my program or focus. Grant me to accept with humor and joy the utter independence of the blowing of your Spirit, to embrace it and abandon myself to its stirring today. For Jesus' sake, Amen.

— Jonathan P. Larson, Atlanta, Georgia

Blooming from Bleakness

"Listen to me, you that pursue righteousness, you that seek the Lord. Look to the rock from which you were hewn, and to the quarry from which you were dug. For the Lord will comfort Zion; the Lord will comfort all her waste places, and will make her wilderness like Eden, her desert like the garden of the Lord; joy and gladness will be found in her, thanksgiving and the voice of song."

—Isaiah 51: 1, 3 (NRSV)

Sometimes we face work situations or people problems so challenging that we feel nothing but frustration and despair. Servant leadership calls for understanding the ways of God and people well enough that we see promise where others may see no hope. Leadership then calls for creating the conditions for that potential to blossom.

It is mid-February and our Pennsylvania landscape remains bleak. I look out to see nothing but snow and naked trees and bushes. But my mother, who has been watching the ways of God's world for 87 years, must see something else. She pulls on her coat and ventures out into that lifeless scene with her old butcher knife. After a time, she returns with an armful of long, unsightly sticks. She fills every spare vase and jar in her warm apartment with these gangly switches.

Two weeks later I again drive through our still-barren countryside to visit Mom. When I walk into her apartment, I am greeted with a burst of indescribable loveliness. Every corner of her home laughs with the brilliant yellow of blooming forsythia!

Ever life-giving God, today give us eyes to see your hope and potential in persons and places many would ignore. Amen.

Faith sees in the soul the blooming flower, while all around the landscape remains bleak.

— Earl Martin, Harrisonburg, Virginia

Dancing Around the "IN" Box

*". . . but if you sow to the Spirit, you will reap eternal
life from the Spirit. So let us not grow weary in doing
what is right, for we will reap at harvest-time, if we
do not give up. So then, whenever we have opportunity, let us work for the good of all . . ."*

— Galatians 6:8b-10 (NRSV)

Have you ever sat down to your desk and felt a moment
of heaviness? Do you ever feel the tedium of the day-in-
day-out demands? Have you ever looked at your full
"IN" box, knowing that all those letters need a response, and
felt a touch of fatigue? Those were my feelings that morning.

But for some unknown reason, I sat quietly a few moments
longer, just staring at the stack of papers. Soon I was lost in that
quiet place of the spirit we sometimes call prayer. Then it happened: I imagined I saw one of the papers in the "IN" box flut-
ter ever so subtly.

Then I saw several tiny fingers wiggling out between the letters and memos. A tiny hand emerged and waved gently toward
me. A tiny head pushed out from between the papers with a
warm and loving smile. And eyes that sparkled looked with
delight into my surprised face.

Then the papers rustled even more, and a whole, tiny person
jumped out onto my desk. Small as he was, I could see it was
Christano, my friend from Indonesia. As I remembered that
there was a letter from Christano in the box, he chuckled and
started to dance a little jig right there on my desk.

The papers stirred again, and soon out jumped a miniature
Siegfried, one of our board members. He greeted Christano and
joined him in the dance. And then with a flourish came

Roberta, my counterpart from another agency. Ann, my administrative assistant, jumped out with a hoot and joined the fun. Soon a whole troupe of tiny dancers spilled out and started circling my "IN" box. They laughed, they sang, and I was overcome!

Later when I thought back to that strange encounter at my desk, I wondered who spiked my Cheerios. But I quietly thanked God's Spirit for giving me new eyes. Eyes to see that behind all the papers we shuffle, behind all those messages on our computer screens, there dance real people, strange and wondrous, all created in the very image of God.

O God, may your dancing Spirit transform the routines of this day from weariness to aliveness. Energize our hearts and awaken our minds. In each person we encounter today—whether directly or vicariously—may we see your face, your image in whom we are all created. Amen.

Could it be that the Great Dancer of the Universe right now taps lightly on the table before us?

— Earl Martin, Harrisonburg, Virginia

Challenged
by Overwhelming Situations

"Rejoice in the Lord always . . . Let your gentleness be known to everyone. The Lord is near. Do not worry about anything, but in everything by prayer and supplication with thanksgiving let your requests be made known to God . . . whatever is true, whatever is honorable, whatever is just, whatever is pure, whatever is pleasing, whatever is commendable, if there is any excellence and if there is anything worthy of praise, think about these things . . . and the God of peace will be with you."

— Philippians 4:4-9 (NRSV)

Recently, my wife and I were in Calcutta, India. The poverty and need of this city of 22 million people were overwhelming at first. The air was blue with smog. We saw people cook, bathe, and sleep on the streets. We were nearly overwhelmed with the poverty.

Our spirits were lifted while we visited Mother Teresa's House of the Destitute and Dying. This is where her program began over 50 years ago. Men and women dying on the streets are brought here. A former banker from Germany welcomed us and, before we left, he asked us to sing for the men in the crowded room. As we sang, he held one of the dying men. Clearly, he had found his place and purpose in life.

The Philippian text gives some guidance for situations that threaten to overwhelm us. It suggests that we rejoice in God's presence. This means recognizing that God is near and hears our requests as we pray.

When Mother Teresa was given more than enough food for the day, she shared it with those in need around her. She said, "God will provide for tomorrow." When asked how she accounted for her success in caring for the needy in more than 50 countries she said simply, "I pray." The text suggests that we are freed from being overwhelmed in a situation when we truly commit our minds and hearts and the future to God. The text says that whatever is honorable, just, pure, pleasing, and commendable, we are to think about. Opportunities will emerge in the situation that before seemed hopeless.

Dear God, we pause in a moment of quietness to ask your spirit to rest upon us. Give us courage to rise to the challenges and not to be overwhelmed by the tasks which we face today. In you, O God, we claim the opportunity to be beacons of light in moments of darkness. Thank you for hearing our prayer. Amen.

God is with you. Continue to follow the example of persons whom you admire. Use the opportunities that are available this day to bring about change and hope.

— Wilmer Martin, Waterloo, Ontario

Making Things New

"Then I saw a new heaven and a new earth; for the first heaven and the first earth had passed away, and the sea was no more. And I saw the holy city, the new Jerusalem, coming down out of heaven from God, prepared as a bride adorned for her husband. And I heard a loud voice from the throne saying, 'See, the home of God is among mortals. He will dwell with them; they will be his peoples, and God himself will be with them; he will wipe every tear from their eyes. Death will be no more; mourning and crying and pain will be no more, for the first things have passed away.' And the one who was seated on the throne said, 'See, I am making all things new.'"

— Revelation 21:1-5a (NRSV)

Until a few years before he became president of South Africa, Nelson Mandela spent 27 years as a political prisoner on Robbin Island off the coast of Cape Town. Since his release, and particularly in his new leadership position, he has maintained that reconciliation between people, especially former enemies, is the only way to create a "new South Africa." As one powerful symbol of that reconciliation, Robbin Island has now been turned into a museum and nature reserve, staffed by former political prisoners and former prison guards. Former enemies have become colleagues in a common venture.

God is constantly creating all things new. Unless we believe that God renews the work of creation each and every day, and that God lives among us, our lives, work, and prayers grow old, accustomed, and tedious. Our world, communities, churches, homes, and board rooms know the mourning, crying, and pain of which John speaks.

At one board meeting a colleague told of how, in one year, hail had wiped out their family's crop, a car accident had claimed the life of a daughter-in-law, and cancer had taken their daughter. God says, "I will wipe away every tear."

What are the "new things" God would create through this organization? This meeting? Here is one example of people who were enabled by God to create new outcomes.

A Christian nurse in the African country of Malawi talked about her colleagues who regularly delivered babies who themselves, or whose mothers, were infected by the AIDS virus. When surgical gloves were not available, they worked barehanded. I asked, "Aren't you afraid to do that?" She replied, "We are terrified, but we can't turn our backs on our people."

Compassionate God, in the middle of the tears and trials of this day, help us to make things new. Grant that we will be:
—in the midst of struggle and in the heat of battle—servants,
—in the midst of violence, oppression, and hatred—prophetic,
—in the midst of hopelessness and pain—hopeful,
—in the midst of compromise—committed,
—in the midst of bondage and fear—liberated,
—in the midst of intimidation and silence—witnessing,
—in the midst of suffering and death—liberating,
—in the midst of failure and disappointment—believing.
In the name of Jesus, Amen.

— adapted from a South African prayer

God's love and compassion are new every morning. They never fail. — Lamentations 3

— Ron Mathies, Ephrata, Pennsylvania

Even the
Smallest Sign of Life

"Then he told this parable: 'A man had a fig tree planted in his vineyard; and he came looking for fruit on it and found none. So he said to the gardener, "See here! For three years I have come looking for fruit on this fig tree, and still I find none. Cut it down! Why should it be wasting the soil?" He replied, "Sir, let it alone for one more year, until I dig around it and put manure on it. If it bears fruit next year, well and good; but if not, you can cut it down."'

— Luke 13:6-9 (NRSV)

While living in Brussels we worshiped with the Spanish Christian Community. This small church was planted by Mennonite missionaries among Spanish immigrants. It flourished for several years, but then some of the strongest leaders returned to start work in Barcelona. The group lost focus and energy. By the time we arrived it was but a handful of people, most of them members of one extended family.

Sunday mornings often ended in tears and recriminations as bad feelings surfaced. Monthly members' meetings were struggles of wills among strong personalities who knew each other a little too well. When things came to the crisis point and several couples made their decision to leave, it seemed only logical that the whole church should disband. The tree was not bearing fruit. Surely we could use our energies better elsewhere.

A weekend retreat was organized to plan for the future. My husband and I attended, intending to say that we, too, would be looking for another church home. But the spirit of the Gardener was tenacious; the tree was not yet dead. A few others were ready to recommit themselves to caring for it. "Give it one more year," they pleaded. "Your help is badly needed here now."

Over the next few years there was a lot of hard digging and fertilizing, not all of it sweet-smelling! Personality conflicts continued, attendance was sporadic, responsibilities seemed never ending. But, oh, the fruit was sweet when it came. We watched Caroline grow from tentative interest and uncertainty to taking an active leadership role. We cheered Martina on as, in her widowhood, she threw off the chains of a long abusive marriage relationship and danced up the mountain toward God. We held onto Juana as she discovered, tentatively, that she, too, was worthy. After a year with us, Erin returned to her church in the U.S. with her spirit rekindled, having learned to pray.

Gracious Gardener, you see possibilities when we see only problems. You see the living sap at the center of the tree when all we can see are the dry bark and empty branches. Teach us to look deeper. Teach us how to nourish even the smallest signs of life into full blossom. Give us patience. Help us to hold on. And thank you, thank you, for the taste of that fruit. Amen.

"Behold, I make all things new." — Revelation 21:5 (RSV)

— Betsy Headrick McCrae, Hanoi, Vietnam

Sitting
by the Pool

"Now in Jerusalem by the Sheep Gate there is a pool, called in Hebrew Beth-zatha, which has five porticoes. In these lay many invalids—blind, lame, and paralyzed. One man was there who had been ill for 38 years. When Jesus saw him lying there and knew that he had been there a long time, he said to him, 'Do you want to be made well?' The sick man answered him, 'Sir, I have no one to put me into the pool when the water is stirred up; and while I am making my way, someone else steps down ahead of me.' Jesus said to him, 'Stand up, take your mat, and walk.' At once the man was made well and he took up his mat and began to walk."

— John 5:2-9 (NRSV)

Ilearned something surprising about myself in a class on meditation. For one week I read this passage from the Gospel of John every morning and evening. I imagined myself at the pool of Beth-zatha. I sat by the pool as an observer, watching Jesus heal those who were obviously sick and paralyzed. I felt comfortable sitting there in the shade of a tree. Suddenly Jesus turned to me and asked, "And do you want to get well?"

I was startled. "Why, I am well. I am here to help others—the sick and the helpless—into the pool. I work for the church. I am healthy, independent, self-sufficient, and I fell quite well most of the time." Why did Jesus ask me?

As I thought about my reaction I discovered my tendency to see the deficiencies of others rather than their capabilities. I was struck by how easy it is to become "needs-focused." How often when I look at others around me do I see only half-full glasses?

While reflecting on this passage I realized that my independence and my self-sufficiency are also disabilities. They are disabilities when they prevent me from seeing others' capabilities, when they discourage me from being more interdependent in my relationships with others. Our self-sufficiency can lead us away from living interdependently with others and from experiencing God's grace in our lives.

Healing God, we confess our need of you. We acknowledge our weaknesses, our disabilities, our need of your sustaining guidance. We pray for eyes to see the capabilities of others and not only their disabilities. Give us eyes that see the best others have to offer. Give us ears that listen to what others say. Give us hands that reach out to help others and hearts that are open to receive help from others. Amen.

— **Lynette Meck, Akron, Pennsylvania**

Jesus Glasses

"When he saw the crowds, he had compassion for them, because they were harassed and helpless, like sheep without a shepherd."
— Matthew 9:36 (NRSV) (also 14:14, 20:34, Luke 15:20 and 13:34)

When I was young I heard the story of a little boy who had lost both legs. To survive, he begged on a street corner. One day he sat propped up against a building with his tin cup and pencils, hoping a few people would buy a pencil for a few nickels or dimes. A man, running to catch the bus, tripped over the boy, knocked him over and sent the tin cup and the few coins sprawling along the sidewalk. Looking ahead, he saw the bus approaching. Looking back he saw the boy lying on the sidewalk.

Quickly he came back, propped the boy up against the building, gathered the coins, and returned the cup to the boy. Just as he started back toward the bus the boy called out to him. "Hey, Mister." The man paused to look back. The boy asked, "Are you Jesus?"

I imagined what it would be like to be mistaken for Jesus. It seemed to me that that would be the most complete compliment one could receive. Several years ago I had an experience which reminded me of that goal.

While I was visiting a facility for the developmentally disabled, my guide and I made our way around a large room. She introduced me to people whose levels of functioning varied from full understanding to total oblivion. My eye caught a young black woman in a wheelchair. I think it was her skin that first caught my eye. It was so smooth and brown and beautiful. As we neared her, I could see her contorted face and the saliva drooling down her chin and onto her bib. As I approached, she extended a deformed hand. I took it, and suddenly realized that she was drawing my hand to her mouth, intending to kiss it. Instinctively I withdrew my hand, repulsed at the thought of having her drool on me.

I knew instantly I had made a huge mistake. I had just lost an opportunity to be "Jesus" to her. I was filled with remorse. Had I been wearing my "Jesus glasses," I would gladly have allowed her to kiss my hand.

As you continue to provide vision and leadership in this place, I encourage you to wear your "Jesus glasses" so that your work, your decisions, and your attitudes reflect the compassion of our Leader.

Gracious God, thank you for calling us to be your workers. Thank you for the work of this place, for a compelling mission and the opportunity to be your hands, your eyes, and your heart as we minister to the needs of those around us. Help each of us to give freely of our time and our talents. Give us wisdom and courage to do what is right. And always, may we see people as you see them, so your compassion can provide the healing touch that makes all of us whole. Amen.

— **Larry W. Nikkel, Wichita, Kansas**

In His Hands

"For thus saith the Lord, 'Ye shall not see wind, neither shall ye see rain: yet that valley shall be filled with water. . .'"

— II Kings 3:17 (KJV)

For many years I prayed that my husband would learn to know and love the Lord. But as time passed, I saw he had no interest in a close relationship to Christ. Yet still I prayed.

One day I heard a sermon about Jehosaphat, King of Judah. His army and their beasts of war were fatigued. There was no water to quench their thirst. After consulting Elisha the prophet of the Lord, they received the hope that they needed. As dawn broke in the camp the next day, the land was filled with water and they all satisfied their thirst. They did not see the wind, nor did they see the rain, yet the water came by the way of Edom.

This passage inspired me to take heart and be strengthened. I was encouraged to know that even though I did not see a change in my husband, I could leave him in God's hands and trust God to work in his life.

On Mother's Day, May 12, 1991, my request was answered. My husband received the Lord's salvation into his heart. Today he is a faithful Christian, serving and winning souls for Christ.

Boards, too, face seemingly hopeless situations. Have you ever wondered where the money would come from for an important project you felt God was calling you to do? Have you wondered if God really hears prayers? Have personnel issues ever become overwhelming?

God does not always answer our prayers in the ways we hope. Often it takes longer than we expect to receive our answers.

This is why we keep praying. This is why we continue to hope. This is why we are so grateful when our prayers are answered.

Heavenly Father, you are our God. Help us to put our eyes on you and not on the things around us. Remind us that you are working among us even though we may not see immediate indications of your work. Amen.

God is at work in our lives—individually and corporately—satisfying our needs in ways we do not always know and cannot anticipate.

— Juana F. Nuñez, Ocoee, Florida

The Agony
and the Ecstasy
of New Beginnings

*"For a long time I have held my peace, I have kept
still and restrained myself; now I will cry out like a
woman in labor, I will gasp and pant . . . I am about
to do a new thing; now it springs forth; do you not
perceive it? I will make a way in the wilderness and
rivers in the desert."*

— Isaiah 42:14; 43:19 (NRSV)

A few years ago, while on an assignment in Durban, my
husband and I were privileged to participate firsthand in
the birth of the "new South Africa." During those final
years and months just prior to the country's first-ever democratic elections in April, 1994, we alternately agonized and exulted
over the daily news bulletins that surrounded the gradual
demise of apartheid and the longed-for birth of a new society.

The day after the elections I wrote, "I feel somewhat drained
but quietly exuberant. It's as though I've participated in a birth
after a lengthy labor and major heart-stopping complications; a
birth requiring expert handling so that life could be born instead
of death; a birth needing miracles of grace and peace at oppor-
tune moments throughout the labor; a birth at last bringing
forth a new child, highly vulnerable and dripping with blood
which had to be shed before new life could be born . . . "

I still tremble at both the intense joy and the devastating sorrow which accompanied that miraculous birth—a birth which
so dramatically changed the lives of all South Africans at every

level of their existence that some could not survive it. (For example, in the months following the elections, there was a substantial increase in suicides and, in the years since then, others have "fallen" due to the corruption of newly-found power.)

Ultimately, the relatively peaceful transition in government counterbalanced some of the sorrow from all the blood that was shed. Yet everyone was grateful that this was a once-in-a-lifetime event; no one wants to go through the agony and ecstasy of that experience again.

Having witnessed that miraculous birth, I now trust more fully that "ways in the wilderness" and "rivers in the desert" will appear. No matter how ordinary our lives, we can all risk letting go of harmful ways of being, in favor of fresh, new ways of living.

God of new birth, give us grace to recognize the new things which need to be born in our personal lives, in our communities, and in our places of work and worship. Give us also the strength and the courage to move through the agony and ecstasy which those new beginnings will inevitably bring our way. For thine is the honour, the power, and the glory, Amen.

"It is out of the dreams which live in the hearts of people that gardens grow, because 'better worlds are born, not made.'"
—Rubem A. Alves

— Leona Dueck Penner, Winnipeg, Manitoba

A Meditation on Stillness

"Be still, and know that I am God!"

— Psalm 46:10a (NRSV)

" . . . but those who wait for the Lord shall renew their strength . . . "

— Isaiah 40:31a (NRSV)

"Many crowds would gather to hear Jesus and to be cured of their diseases. But he would withdraw to deserted places to pray."

— Luke 5:15b, 16 (NRSV)

When I began to realize that my life was becoming a career of Christian service, I became deeply aware of my need to internalize the quiet, revitalizing truth of these words on stillness, waiting, and prayer. But in spite of my best efforts, including some renewing experiences, I became so exhausted that I decided to resign from my job. I've given myself an extended, unpaid sabbatical from church-related work. For the last three months I've been steadfastly saying no to speaking engagements in favor of reading, writing, and just being in the stillness of a summer garden. Already I feel much better both spiritually and physically.

For a few moments, let go if you can of all activity and quiet your body. Become aware of your breathing until you feel an inner stillness. Then listen to God speak to you, the ancient words of so long ago: "Be still and know that I am God."

Stillness, the Psalmist suggests, comes before we can know God. But how do we find stillness in our over-stimulated lives, our busyness, our zest for speed and efficiency? We all know the awkwardness of silence, whether we worship publicly or privately. We all know the temptation to rush to fill silences with words. Yet we must practice stillness if we are to be of service to others. Without it, we put ourselves—instead of God—at the center and begin to think that everything depends on us. We soon overextend ourselves, and our spirits wither and die.

We have to relearn stillness. We must search for it diligently. Our search may at times even require giving up all that we have so that we once again become "poor in spirit," ready to acknowledge our need of God.

For a few moments now, let us each listen quietly within and reflect on where we are in our journeys toward this stillness which leads us to God.

Silent prayer.

"True silence is the search of wo/man for God . . . "
—Catherine de Hueck Doherty

— **Leona Dueck Penner, Winnipeg, Manitoba**

Courage to Risk

"Be strong and of good courage, and act. Do not be afraid or dismayed; for the Lord God, my God, is with you."

— I Chronicles 28:20 (NRSV)

"Wait for the Lord; be strong and let your heart take courage; wait for the Lord."

— Psalm 27:14 (NRSV)

"Better is the end of a thing than its beginning; the patient in spirit are better than the proud in spirit."

— Ecclesiastes 7:8 (NRSV)

O nce a big building was burning out of control. The building stood at the foot of a long hill and enclosed a large courtyard. Several fire trucks were unable to put out the blaze. Then another fire truck appeared on the scene, crashed recklessly through the burning building, set up in the courtyard, and promptly put out the fire. The onlookers were amazed. The firemen were instant heroes. The owner gave them a contribution in appreciation of their efforts. When asked what they planned to do with the money the Chief replied, "We will fix the brakes on our fire truck!"

Boards and managers are reluctant to make changes. Outcomes are always uncertain, and leaders want to avoid the embarrassment of failure. To discern what is a reasonable risk and what is a foolhardy gamble is what board service is all about. It starts by deciding if the information on hand is adequate to make a wise decision.

Often a deadline is calling for a decision before the necessary information can be gathered. Sometimes the call for more information is justified; board members should not allow themselves to be pushed into a decision prematurely. Sometimes a request for more data is pure procrastination.

Boards face a hard choice when a promising idea shows signs of faltering. Wisdom is required to know when to cut losses. The proud in spirit are often inclined to stop prematurely to avoid embarrassment. On the other hand, a fear of failure may lead to postponing the evil day while the effort is allowed to stumble on. Pride complicates decision-making.

Lord, give us the courage to make changes which involve risk and the grace to accept failure when the end is not better than the beginning. Give us the daring to risk yet another venture. Amen.

Nothing risked, nothing gained. A business or organization which has never experienced a setback has probably not taken sufficient risks.

— Vern Preheim, North Newton, Kansas

Let's Begin With Prayer

"Be still and know that I am God."

— Psalm 46:10a (NRSV)

Yes, it's radical and—perhaps—impractical? Or is it the only way to cope in today's world? After nearly a decade of working in a Christian organization, I've come to believe that every meeting should begin with some quiet time and/or prayer. Every meeting. No matter its size, no matter its agenda, no matter its mix of people. God calls us to be still in our lives and in our busyness.

To be still and know, and to pray, helps each of us to achieve perspective. Yes, we can catch our individual and collective breaths, but to be still and know sets the stage for love, for harmony, and for letting God in. Then each person present is calmer, more at peace, and more ready to listen to and discuss with others. It's also healthy. All of us are rushed. Pressed. Without one millisecond of relief in our Information Age. Stress dogs us.

Silence and prayer definitely prepare us when controversial issues—or confrontations—lie ahead. I have often rushed into a meeting to find electric tensions, to find everyone hearing that so-and-so will "go at it." A wise chairperson or an attendee would sensitively suggest, "Let's begin with prayer." Such an act can transform a room. Tough words and opinions may still be voiced, disagreements aired, and hurts and angers expressed, but with respect and, often, love. It can happen, even when differences seem most irreconcilable and in the most inescapable rock-and-hard-place situations.

What if the meeting includes people of different faiths or those without faith? What about persons who don't care for prayer? Give everyone space. Open by suggesting, "Let us be quiet and still for a few moments. I will lead a prayer, but if prayer is not your approach or preference, please meditate or observe quietly while we pray. For a few moments we will be still, we will be quiet, we will be 'in community.'"

(after a brief silence)

We thank you Lord for this gathering, for this opportunity to serve you. We ask you blessings upon this meeting and everyone here and the matters we are to discuss. May we act in wisdom, in love, and to your glory. We have prepared for this time as much as we can. We now surrender our meeting to you. Amen.

— Jim Purks, Americus, Georgia

Functioning with Low Visibility

"Now faith is the assurance of things hoped for, the conviction of things not seen. For by it, men of old received divine approval. By faith we understand that the world was created by the word of God, so that what is seen was made out of things that did not appear. By faith Abel . . . by faith Enoch . . . without faith it is impossible to please him."

— Hebrews 11:1, 2, 4, 5, 6 (RSV)

Vera Randall, international businesswoman, tells the story of her teenage son Tim entering the famed Hawkesbury Classic Kayak race in Australia. Initially dismissing his interest as fleeting, youthful exuberance, she knew he was serious when he used his own hard-earned money to buy a kayak and a how-to manual. After months of rigorous training, Tim faced the day of the big race. After enduring scrutinizing and briefing sessions, all 400 contestants, some of them wily veterans, set out on the 70-mile, all-night race.

Vera served as Tim's land crew, traveling by car to checkpoints along the winding Hawkesbury River. At midnight word came through the radio that Tim's group was approaching the half-way point. The night was dark and foggy. Listening carefully, Vera could hear paddles dipping in and out of water. When she was able to recognize the lead kayaker, Vera was surprised to see that it was Tim. Weary with exhaustion and muscles aching, he came ashore for some sandwiches, hot soup, and a vigorous shoulder massage. Then he was back into the tortuous second half of the race, full of determination.

Vera moved to the finish line. Glancing at her watch intermittently, she tried in vain to sleep away the hours. Finally she joined the hundreds of other bleary-eyed land crew members on the riverbank. Thirteen hours after the start of the race the lead paddles came round the last bend of the river as the sun struggled to break through the morning fog. As they approached . . . she blinked wearily . . . she saw that Tim was the winner.

In a post-race interview he was asked if the fog had hindered the race. "Not really," was his reply. "I went as far as I could see, and when I got there I could see further."

Tim's observation applies to board work as much as it does to Australian kayak-racing. Directors are seldom able to see the end from the beginning. They cannot wait for the fog to lift. They are required to operate in limited visibility, never sure of the outcome. Only those who go as far as they can see, with faith that when they get there they will be able to see further, are eligible to win the race.

God of Abraham and Rahab, we acknowledge that the race is not always to the swift. The race of life is won by those who have faith to see them through times of uncertainty. It is in those dark moments of the night that your presence and invisible guidance is most needed. Grant us enabling faith so that we are eligible to receive the reward awaiting those who seek to do your will. Amen.

— **Vera Randall (with Edgar Stoesz), Dural, Australia**

Surrendering Our Rights;
Asserting Our Responsibilities

*"He has brought down rulers from their thrones but
has lifted up the humble."*

— Luke 1:52 (NIV)

Following the successful planting and shepherding of a lively, growing church in the Rocky Mountains, Pat was invited to take the post of senior pastor in a large, prosperous church in the Midwest. The congregation was a conservative post in a somewhat liberal mainline denomination. Pat considered the offer a plum.

After taking the position, Pat began to see a different side of the church. Powerful and influential elders held a firm rule over the affairs of the church, not allowing him to exercise the kind of spiritual and administrative leadership which brought him such success before. Then he discovered that many on the Board of Elders, as well as his own staff, were angry about certain denominational social and doctrinal positions and wanted him to lead the church out of the denomination. There was little joy in this congregation.

What had he stepped into? Pat searched his heart and tried to remember God's call on his life. He sensed that God wanted this church to remain in the denomination as salt and light. As a result, Pat and his wife suffered rebuke and isolation from many who they thought were close friends. Some took him out to lunch and suggested that he resign. He resolved not to accuse and blame, but in humility to turn the other cheek and to seek reasoned solutions and accommodations. An excellent preacher, he never used the pulpit to participate in the political fray.

After a very painful year, what at first appeared to be a majority of dissidents turned out to be a vocal minority, and they left the church. In the following year, Pat felt the freedom to use his spiritual and administrative gifts. A wonderful spirit entered the congregation, and they started to experience unusual joy for the first time in years. God honored this pastor who was willing to submit to unfair abuse with a gracious spirit for the higher good of love and unity.

Father, show us daily how to let go of the attention and respect we think we deserve so that we can get on with the high calling of being your humble servants. Help us to bring healing and reconciliation to a divided and angry world. Amen.

Thomas More wrote, "Humility, that low, sweet root from which all heavenly virtues shoot." What is God waiting to do in my life if I would only step aside, giving him room to work his wonders?

— Lance Renault, Greenville, South Carolina

Walking by Faith
When the Future
Is Uncertain

"Know therefore that the Lord your God is God; he is the faithful God, keeping his covenant of love to a thousand generations of those who love him and keep his commands."

— Deuteronomy 7:9 (NIV)

For almost 50 years American Leprosy Missions (ALM) has supported leprosy treatment and rehabilitation services in the west African nation of Angola. In the early years, when Angola was still a Portuguese colony, the most effective treatment programs were done by Christian missions, assisted by ALM. There was, however, no cure in those days, and progress was slow.

In the early 1980s a cure was found for leprosy. Many governments in endemic countries adopted the new treatment regimen and redoubled their efforts to find persons still being infected by this dreaded disease. However, following independence from Portugal, Angola was thrown into civil war, making it impossible to set up a national leprosy control program. The protracted war also hampered the medical work of Christian missions. Medical facilities which escaped bombing or looting were finding their caseloads taken up by numerous leg injuries and amputations resulting from the multitude of land mines.

So severe were the obstacles resulting from poverty, compounded by war, that ALM considered pulling out of Angola. Tempted to shift its resources to more hospitable countries,

ALM finally chose to stay, hoping conditions would improve. For years, a simple sense of mission, not grand plans, kept ALM at work in this tortured country.

Then several things happened in 1996 that could be attributed only to answered prayer. The warring factions declared peace. ALM was able to sign a unique agreement with the Ministry of Health for implementing a national leprosy control program in conjunction with church-based efforts. And a talented young Swiss doctor who grew up in Angola agreed to return there to coordinate ALM's expanded government and church leprosy programs. After almost 50 years, an effective national leprosy control program, with a broad-based Christian witness, was now in sight.

Father, help us to stay the course when we know what we do is right in your eyes, yet the future is uncertain and we see no fruit. Whether the waters be stormy or at dead calm, we trust that you are directing us to the safe harbor and glad land you have waiting for us over the horizon. Amen.

We know that God, out of his abundant love, is faithful to the believer. May we be as faithful to him out of our trust in his abundant promises.

— Lance Renault, Greenville, South Carolina

Am I
My Brother's Keeper?

*"Now Abel kept flocks, and Cain worked the soil . . .
Cain brought some of the fruits of the soil as an offering to the Lord. But Abel brought fat portions from
some of the firstborn of his flock. The Lord looked
with favor on Abel for his offering, but on Cain and
his offering he did not look with favor. So Cain was
very angry . . . Then the Lord said to Cain, 'Where is
your brother Abel?' 'I don't know,' he replied. 'Am I
my brother's keeper?'"*

— Genesis 4:2-9 (NIV)

Cain kills his brother Abel in a jealous snit, the Creator
God wants to know what happened, and Cain responds
cynically, "Am I my brother's keeper?" In the world of
charity, that question is at the crux. To those wishing to avoid
responsibility, the answer is no. For those wishing to broaden
and share responsibility, the answer inevitably is yes.

One of the most unsettling and stunning experiences one can
have is to visit the Holocaust Memorial Museum in
Washington, D.C. From medical instruments used to measure
"racial purity," to videos of death camps and voices of survivors,
it is a wrenching twist on Cain's epithet . . . and a haunting
reminder that we are intrinsically tied to our brothers and sisters throughout the world.

One room at the Holocaust Museum is devoted to those
"righteous Gentiles" who cared. My favorite is a Greek
Orthodox Archbishop, ordered by the Nazis to provide a list of
all Jews in the area. He agreed, and the next day he returned

with the list. It had one name on it—his own. He saw clearly that he did have a God-given responsibility for others that he could not shake or escape. Who he was, what he believed, and how he acted were shaped by his desire, his calling, to keep or care for his brother and sister Jews. Their Jewishness did not divorce him from their kinship with him.

Yes, we are our brothers' keepers. Sometimes we wonder if they are worth it, if they are worthy. But God's challenge to us has nothing to do with anyone else's worthiness. God looks at us as at Cain and asks, "Why are you angry?" To us God might say, "Why are you put out, frustrated, cynical, weary from being your brother's keeper?" God pushes us in verse 7 to "do what is right."

Despite our rugged individualism, our belief in personal accountability, our pride in pulling ourselves up by our bootstraps, the Judeo-Christian ethic still stands—we are our brothers' keepers, we do have a share, a stake, in each other.

For those who have cared for us, O Lord, for those who have helped us along the way, for those who accepted being our keepers, for those who did not turn away, we give thanks, and seek the patience to do as well for others. Amen.

— **David Johnson Rowe, Pittsfield, Massachusetts**

Something Small
for God

*"Bless the Lord, O my soul! O Lord my God, thou art
very great! Thou art clothed with honor and majesty,
who coverest thyself with light as with a garment,
who has stretched out the heavens like a tent, who
has laid the beams of thy chambers on the waters,
who makes the clouds thy chariot, who ridest on the
wings of the wind, who makest the winds thy mes-
sengers, fire and flame thy ministers."*

— Psalm 104:1-4 (RSV)

We may have two contrasting feelings as we try to do
our best. We tend either to get so caught up in our
own project or idea that everything else seems
insignificant, or the size of the situation facing us overwhelms
us so that we feel insignificant. We need perspective.

In Alex Haley's *Roots*, when Kunta Kinte is born in Africa,
his father takes the infant outside and lifts the fragile, helpless
new life up to the heavens of God and says to the child,
"Behold, the only thing greater than yourself!" What a wonderful view with which to begin each step of life!

Paradoxically, but not in contradiction, the Psalmist reminds
Little Us of the absolute, majestic, unparalleled greatness of
God. Why? To make us feel small, inadequate, insignificant?
No! The Psalmist wants us to understand the greatness of our
Divine Partner in all we do.

With God at our side, nothing we do is insignificant or unim-
portant. As we work with God, everything we do has value, and
we are valuable. It is not fame or size or acclaim we seek.

Instead, doing what God needs to have done makes every effort significant.

When my sister and her husband worked in Zaire they befriended a young woman who was blind. Some Italian missionary nurses were convinced that if she were to have an operation in Italy, her sight could be restored. My sister started raising funds for the operation. Many responded negatively, asking, "Do you know how many blind people there are in the world? What use is it to help just one?" Donna's response was simple: "This is the one I know I can help."

Large, national, or even world, issues can be depressing—hunger, homelessness, poverty, for example. But hunger is beaten by one meal at a time, homelessness by one house or even one brick at a time, poverty by one job or one chance at a time.

Think of the stunning miracle of the multiplication of the fishes and loaves. Jesus was offered too few fish and too little bread. But something small, given to God, becomes wonderfully abundant with God. To set that miracle in motion, however, someone had to offer what appeared to be insignificant.

God, I give you my first thought, my first deed, my first step, as a humble offering, counting on you to take it, use it, and work miracles with it. Amen.

With God, mustard-seed-size faith can move mountains.

— David Johnson Rowe, Pittsfield, Massachusetts

Trust
in the Lord

"Trust in the Lord with all your heart and do not rely on your own insight. In all your ways acknowledge him, and he will make straight your paths."

— Proverbs 3:5,6 (NRSV)

Our church had just finished celebrating its 150th anniversary. Prompted by that event and the approach of the new millennium we had renewed our commitment to our Nissan statement and dreamed of what we might be or do in the next century.

We had a new pastor who was overworked but respected by all, a vacancy instead of a part-time director of Christian education, and an organization of volunteers that drew good people, but never enough. The structure seemed a bit stuffy and lacked the energy required to make our dreams a reality. Being a Congregational Church (UCC) we, of course, were rational, democratic, and deliberate. (We were also in a deficit budget year.)

As Chair of the Leadership Committee I was charged with reviewing both our staffing and volunteer structures. With the help of a facilitator, we spent months looking at all aspects of our church organization. I was preparing for a final meeting; it was decision-making time! For my daily reading I had begun Proverbs and just that morning was struck by Proverbs 3:5, 6, verses my father had often cited in conversation and correspondence.

I conducted the meeting, giving time to discuss each staffing model. Should we hire a part-time Associate Minister to work with our Pastor? My assumption was that our congregation would not assume an additional $40,000 salary when our current deficit was $28,000.

It was clear from the first few comments that there was a strong will to meet the new opportunities for ministry by taking a risk; that is, hiring a part-time associate. As I pressed for more conservative approaches without pushing my point of view too hard, I began to remember Proverbs 3:5, 6 and could not help but share my morning reading with the group.

The vote was unanimous! We soon will have a full-time Associate Pastor!

Dear Lord, we confess our temptation to listen to others, but to press on, convinced that our way is more mature, more experienced, and best reasoned. Keep us open to your direction. May we put you first, and may we seek the wisdom of others to whom you minister. Amen.

At times God speaks to us through others.

— Warren Sawyer, Swampscott, Massachusetts

Prayer
of the Heart

"In all my prayers for all of you, I always pray with joy because of your partnership in the gospel from the first day until now, being confident of this, that he who began a good work in you will carry it on to completion until the day of Christ Jesus . . . And this is my prayer: that your love may abound more and more in knowledge and depth of insight, so that you may be able to discern what is best and may be pure and blameless until the day of Christ, filled with the fruit of righteousness that comes through Jesus Christ—to the glory and praise of God."

— Philippians 1: 4-6, 9-11 (NIV)

The late Henri Nouwen, one of the 20th century's greatest teachers on spirituality, believed that meeting God in solitude and silence is essential if we want to unite our lives with the will of God. In his 1981 book, *The Way of the Heart,* he wrote: "Solitude is the place where Christ remodels us in his own image and frees us from the victimizing compulsions of the world. Solitude is the place of our salvation."

That saving solitude is hard for most of us to find. Burdened by the world's expectations and lured by its enticements, we seldom get quiet enough to listen to the Spirit. But when we do, we tap into the source of strength for Christian ministry—what Henri Nouwen called the "prayer of the heart." This kind of prayer touches our souls, not merely our minds. "The prayer of the heart," he wrote, "is a prayer that does not allow us to limit our relationship with God to interesting words or pious emotions. Such prayer transforms our whole being into Christ."

Nouwen encouraged simple prayers—such as "Jesus, master, have mercy on me"—so we don't get distracted by trying to find the right words. "Such a simple, easily repeated prayer can slowly empty out our crowded interior life and create the quiet space where we dwell with God," he wrote. "It can be like a ladder along which we can descend into the heart and ascend to God."

Simple prayers, said often, eventually fulfill the biblical command to pray without ceasing. "The prayer continues to pray within me even as I talk with others or concentrate on manual labor," Nouwen wrote. "The prayer has become the active presence of God's spirit guiding me through life." Henri Nouwen's prayer was that his heart would become one with God's. What great things might God enable us to do if we learned to pray like that?

Lord, we come to you in silence, out of a noisy world. We confess we do not listen for your voice as often as we should. We ask that you would quiet our hearts. We want a silent space to dwell with you. In this quiet moment, we seek your transforming presence. Guide our hearts and minds toward your will and purpose. Amen.

Before we can follow God's path, we need to stop and ask for God's directions.

— **Paul Schrag, Newton, Kansas**

But the Greatest of These
Is Hope

"Jesus said to them again, 'Peace be with you. As the Father has sent me, even so I send you.'"

— John 20:21 (NRSV)

When I served in Honduras in the 1980s, I was grateful for many opportunities to worship with the Honduran Mennonites and see the Bible through their eyes.

I once heard Lucas Bonilla of the Honduran Mennonite Church give a devotional to a study tour. He quoted Jesus after the resurrection, speaking to his disciples, "Peace be with you. As the Father has sent me, so I send you." Then he asked, "How did God send Jesus?" There could be many responses, but the one Lucas was looking for was that God sent Jesus into a situation of conflict in which his life was threatened from the time of his birth. Jesus taught his followers how to be disciples in the midst of conflict.

Jesus knew what his mission was to be. He identified it in Luke 4:18, 19: "The Spirit of the Lord is upon me, because he has anointed me to preach good news to the poor . . ." In Jesus' day this was a controversial mission; for the Honduran Mennonites it still is.

Lucas concluded his devotional with I Corinthians 13:13: "So faith, hope, love abide, these three; but the greatest of these is love." "In our context," he remarked, "we place the emphasis on hope. We have hope that God has something to say about the socio-political needs of Central America. God has placed us in this situation of conflict. It is our responsibility, our challenge to respond."

Recently while traveling in Africa I found similar themes in a speech given by J.N.K. Mugambi, a Kenyan professor. He wrote: "Hope is a psychological necessity for the healthy maintenance of human community and individuality. Without hope, life cannot be sustained. Hope makes all the difference. St. Paul teaches that there is a very close correlation between faith, hope, and love. We can say that faith is the cement which binds love and hope. Love is the relationship which makes life possible—which generates life. Without love there can be no life. Without hope, life cannot be sustained. Without faith, there is no love to generate and no hope to sustain life." (*The Church of Africa: Towards a Theology of Reconstruction*, 1991)

Lord, we thank you for the privilege of working with you to build a better world. We ask that you encourage us with your hope and that you help us to understand the importance of hope for all the people. As we have heard from Latin America and Africa, it is hope that sustains life and that motivates people to move forward to improve their lives and those of their neighbors'. May we give and receive hope freely, knowing that the sharing of hope knows no bounds. Amen.

When people are hopeful, they will capably solve many problems themselves.

— **Linda Shelly, Lancaster, Pennsylvania**

Abraham and the "Vision Thing"

"By faith Abraham obeyed when he was called to set out for a place that he was to receive as an inheritance; and he set out, not knowing where he was going. By faith he stayed for a time in the land he had been promised, as in a foreign land, living in tents, as did Isaac and Jacob, who were heirs with him of the same promise. For he looked forward to the city that has foundations, whose architect and builder is God. By faith he received power of procreation, even though he was too old—and Sarah herself was barren—because he considered him faithful who had promised. Therefore from one person, and this one as good as dead, descendants were born, as many as the stars of heaven and as innumerable as grains of sand by the seashore."

— Hebrews 11:8-12 (NRSV)

Vision is the first requirement of leadership. But we live in a culture that is hard on visionaries. We bemoan the fact that our political leaders are singularly lacking in vision, yet the climate is such that leaders hesitate to lead. Politicians are creatures of the political system who survive and get to the top only by conforming to its demands. We have become cynical about leaders who try to sell themselves rather than calling us to a great cause.

We also know that we do indeed perish—as groups and as individuals—when there is no vision, no dream that lifts us above the mundane. Churches and Christian organizations can show the way. The Holy Spirit gives certain individuals vision. This gift is given to enhance witness and enliven the Christian community. The community has an important role to play in cultivating respect for the work of the Spirit by being open to the visionary.

Abraham was a visionary. He did not try to sell a vision; he lived a vision and followed a call. This is the mark of a true visionary.

Gracious God, give us the confidence of Abraham to follow you. Attune our ears so that we will hear when you call. Transform our barrenness into fruitfulness that glorifies your name and blesses the nations. Amen.

Vision is life-giving. It makes the impossible possible, the unthinkable thinkable.

— **Wilbert R. Shenk, Pasadena, California**

Certainty
Versus Faith

"Now faith is the assurance of things hoped for, the conviction of things not seen. Indeed, by faith our ancestors received approval. By faith we understand that the worlds were prepared by the word of God, so that what is seen was made from things that are not visible. By faith Abel offered to God a more acceptable sacrifice than Cain's. Through this he received approval as righteous, God himself giving approval to his gifts; he died, but through his faith he still speaks. By faith Enoch was taken so that he did not experience death; and 'he was not found, because God had taken him.' For it was attested before he was taken away that 'he had pleased God.' And without faith it is impossible to please God, for whoever would approach him must believe that he exists and that he rewards those who seek him. By faith Noah, warned by God about events as yet unseen, respected the warning and built an ark to save his household; by this he condemned the world and became an heir to the righteousness that is in accordance with faith."

— Hebrews 11:1-7 (NRSV)

What right do we have to expect decisions taken by a board, itself an expression of modern organization—rational, controlled by carefully developed policies, bureaucratically managed—to be faith-filled? Faith-based? Faith seems airy-fairy—"the assurance of things hoped for"—wishful thinking. Yet I have seen it happen!

The most satisfying decisions are those that require a leap of faith and that take us into uncharted territory. It is these leaps-of-faith decisions that set new directions and result in surprising fruitfulness.

Responsible and disciplined administration can assist in realizing the fruits of faith-based decisions, but operating only within the boundaries set by established precedent and policy is stifling. This binds a board or committee to the certainties of the past. But if we are seeking to do God's work by following God's way, we are called to be pilgrims and sojourners. Faith calls us to go beyond the present, to move toward God's goal for us.

God of surprises, surprise us today with fresh insight and courage so that we dare to follow you in paths we have not walked before. We confess we like the comfort of the known and predictable. Give us faith to trust you and thereby become "heirs of righteousness that is in accordance with faith." Amen.

Certainty cannot produce faith; it produces only frantic assertion. The fruit of faith is confidence in God, the author of faith.

— Wilbert R. Shenk, Pasadena, California

Finding Strength
in God

"Now the Amalekites had raided the Negev and Ziklag. They had attacked Ziklag and burned it, and had taken captive the women and all who were in it, both young and old. They killed none of them, but carried them off as they went on their way. When David and his men came to Ziklag, they found it destroyed by fire and their wives and sons and daughters taken captive. So David and his men wept aloud until they had no strength left to weep. David's two wives had been captured—Ahinoam of Jezreel and Abigail, the widow of Nabal of Carmel. David was greatly distressed because the men were talking of stoning him; each one was bitter in spirit because of his sons and daughters. But David found strength in the Lord his God."

— I Samuel 30:1-6 (NIV)

There are times in the life of every leader when all human resources for support and encouragement are stripped away. Tough decisions must be made; the road ahead is lonely. No one else seems to understand the steps which must be taken. At those precise moments the experience of David points us to the last line of defense.

David turned directly to God. Consider the situation. He had left unprotected his wives and family, as well as his soldiers'. Now everything was lost! Every home was destroyed and their dependents were all taken captive, maybe forever. His men had wept their hearts out, and then became bitter toward him.

David had no human recourse. He took the one remaining step he knew. He turned to God and took courage from the one who had always kept him. In that confidence, David triumphed. He followed the enemy and recovered everything.

The key to effective Christian leadership is conscious dependence on God. How frequently is the darkest moment just before dawn? While at Rosedale Bible Institute, I led the staff in a decision to invite the constituency to pray—just pray—for funds for a new staff house. We did so, but the needed resources seemed to be coming far too slowly. We were tempted to reverse our decision and appeal for funds in a more familiar pattern. We felt vulnerable. What if we prayed and the funds never came? However, we decided to persevere, and in the next weeks we saw the glory of God. A surprise telephone call from one donor met the whole need. We were suddenly over the top!

David found strength in the Lord his God. So may we.

Thank you, God, that you are here for us. Thank you that it is not what we see, but who we do not see that makes all the difference. We turn to you. In faith we turn our eyes away from human resources and fix them on you. We remember your faithfulness to us in the past. We trust you for the future! Amen.

God takes full responsibility for those who trust him wholly.

— Richard Showalter, Salunga, Pennsylvania

Tears of Tragedy,
Songs of Joy

"When the Lord restored the fortunes of Zion, we were like those who dream. Then our mouth was filled with laughter, and our tongue with shouts of joy; then it was said among the nations, 'The Lord has done great things for them.' The Lord has done great things for us, and we rejoiced. Restore our fortunes, O Lord, like the watercourses in the Negeb. May those who sow in tears reap with shouts of joy. Those who go out weeping, bearing the seed for sowing, shall come home with shouts of joy, carrying their sheaves."

— Psalm 126 (NRSV)

Worldwide, more people suffer from depression than any other mental illness. Eventually we all encounter tragedies that dash our most cherished dreams and turn our fondest hopes into profound sorrow. The grief following a loss can plunge us into depression and its accompanying mental, emotional, and spiritual numbness.

In 1996 my 25-year-old niece—a bright doctoral student who had dedicated her life to serving others through scientific research—was randomly abducted from her automobile. For more than two months thousands of Christians over North America prayed that she might be released unharmed. However, when her murdered body was found, we felt deep anguish because God had not answered our fervent prayers.

The Israelites, no doubt, experienced depression after they had been carried away to Babylon. This unhappy band of captives wept bitterly on the banks of the city's rivers. When

Cyrus, king of Persia, allowed these exiles to return home to Jerusalem many years later, they were overjoyed. "Our mouths were filled with laughter, our tongues with songs of joy," notes the Psalmist. "The Lord has done great things for us, and we are filled with joy." God had answered their prayers.

When tragedy strikes, we can spiral downward into an unfathomable pit of despair. When our children reject Christian values, when our best friends betray our trust, when death separates us forever from a loved one, we want to go to the river and cry our hearts out. When searing adversity strikes, we lament, "Where is God? Why has He failed us?"

Just at the moment when we are tempted to abandon our faith, God can connect with us in unexpected ways. Committed Christians extend God's compassion through caring words and kind deeds. God's word also provides assurance of ongoing love. God declares through the Psalmist, "Those who sow in tears will reap with songs of joy. He who goes out weeping, carrying seeds to sow, will return with songs of joy, carrying sheaves with him."

When tragedy strikes, O God, show us your face. Help us feel your heart of compassion. Take away our tears, and through your Holy Spirit breathe into us songs of joy. Through Jesus Christ, who inspires hope for life eternal, Amen.

God can revive our flagging spirits and renew our hope. Hallelujah!

— Stuart W. Showalter, Goshen, Indiana

Even Eagles Need Faith

"As an eagle stirreth up her nest, fluttereth over the young, spreadeth abroad her wings, taketh them, beareth them on her wings. . ."

— Deuteronomy 32:11 (also Isaiah 40:31) (KJV)

L ife is full of critical moments for both individuals and organizations. Some of those times are pleasant, some are joyous, some are filled with fear, some require faith.

High in the mountains on a rocky cliff, the mother eagle knows it is time for her young to take wing and fly. She begins nudging them to the edge of the nest. Hundreds of feet below is the bubbling stream. Her heart quickens. Why is there always resistance as the eaglets begin this phase of their lives? Can they not sense the glory of soaring?

Flying must be learned, even by eagles! It is their ultimate reality. They must leave the nest if they are ever to feel the rapturous updrafts that will carry them high above the earth. Why is it so difficult to leave the nest? Don't they know that soaring begins with overcoming fear?

As the day of testing the eaglets' wings arrives, the mother eagle is anxious. Maybe her young won't fly. Maybe the air will not support one of their wings. Her role is not only to bring life from the egg, but to teach her young to survive. She must help them fly or die.

In God's plan, certain achievements begin with an act of faith. Mother eagle draws on her God-given instincts and nudges the eaglets to the edge of the nest. Her heart beats rapidly as she moves to fulfill this task. One by one she pushes them from the nest. One by one they begin to fly—first hesitantly; then with confidence!

So in our lives—we have been the recipients of God's greatest gift. However, before we can soar, before we can receive this great gift, before we can begin our journey with the Master, we must step out in faith and believe.

Doing even the simple and the obvious takes faith, but those steps can take on great meaning. If we are to soar like eagles, if we are to experience rapturous uplifts to God or the delicacies of spiritual life, we must begin by stepping out in faith.

Great God, maker of heaven and earth, creator of eagles and all of life, forgive our doubts and fears. Forgive us when we shrink from doing what you expect of us. Give the experienced among us the faith of the mother eagle. Help those of us who are inexperienced to step out in faith and find our wings to do your work. Amen.

— **Ben Sprunger, Washington, Ohio**

Failure
in Perspective

"Feed the hungry! Help those in trouble! Then your light will shine out from the darkness, and the darkness around you shall be as bright as day. And the Lord will guide you continually, and satisfy you with all good things, and keep you healthy, too: And you will be like a well-watered garden, like an ever flowing spring. Your sons will rebuild the long deserted ruins of your cities, and you shall be known as The People Who Rebuilt Their Walls and Cities."

— Isaiah 58:10-12 (TLB)

D r. Ida Scudder's missionary career spanned more than 50 years. If the title "iron woman" was ever deserved, she earned it. One of the first women to graduate from an American medical college (Cornell, in 1899), Dr. Ida devoted her life to India's sick and dying. She founded, among other things, the Vellore Medical Center in south India, now a bustling, sprawling facility covering several city blocks.

Yet it was this accomplished woman who said, "I attribute what success I have had . . . to my failures. Yes, I mean just that. We learn very little . . . from success. Success feeds ego; failure chastens it. Success makes you look up, and the sun dazzles your eyes; failure causes you to look down, and you mind your step. Those who can fail and learn, who can try and fall and get up and go on, who can make a new start and be defeated and still go on, are the ones who succeed in the end."

Milton Hershey went through numerous bankruptcies before he perfected the recipe that led to the famous Hershey Bar.

Michael Jordan, arguably the greatest basketball player ever, did not make his high school team his sophomore year. Mickey Mantle struck out 710 times. Emily Dickinson wrote about 1,800 poems, but only seven were published in her lifetime. The Apostle Peter recovered from his embarrassing lapse at the crucifixion to preach a great sermon at Pentecost.

Dear God, help us not to be destroyed by our failures, but to learn from them. Help us not to relax and gloat when we are up, nor to grovel in discouragement when we are down. Give us strength to pursue our mission even when the outcome is in doubt. Grant us a living faith that will see us through troubled times, for we remind ourselves that the work is thine. We mean to be worthy servants in your vineyard. Amen.

"Success feeds ego; failure chastens it. Success makes you look up, and the sun dazzles your eyes; failure causes you to look down, and you mind your step." —Ida Scudder

— Edgar Stoesz, Akron, Pennsylvania

To God
Be the Glory

*"O the depth of the riches and wisdom and knowl-
edge of God! How unsearchable are his judgments
and how inscrutable his ways! 'For who has known
the mind of the Lord, or who has been his counselor?'
'Or who has given a gift to him that he might be
repaid?' For from him and through him and to him
are all things. To him be glory for ever."*
— Romans 11:33-36 (RSV) (also Matthew 5:14-16)

Before retiring as Executive Secretary of Mennonite Central Committee (MCC), Orie Miller was determined to see a program established in Haiti. "So near, and so poor," were his words. At age 28, I was totally unprepared when I was asked to undertake this assignment. It was my first year at MCC; it was his last. First I located Haiti on the map; then I read about it in the library. Some days later I asked Miller, "What can we expect to do for a country so poor?"

"Not much," was his surprising response. Seeing my puzzlement he added, "But it will do a lot for us." I was shocked and disappointed. Confused! The thought of going there to help ourselves seemed totally wrong. What is more, my reading and youthful idealism tempted me to try something heroic. The term "Operation Bootstrap" was being used then to describe the strong recovery in neighboring Puerto Rico. Why not something like that in Haiti?

Forty years later I have concluded Miller was right—twice. The lives of literally hundreds of talented and dedicated MCC workers who have served there since have been immeasurably enriched. For many it was a life-changing experience. At the same time, in an ultimate sense, we cannot claim to have done much for Haiti. We tried—goodness knows, we tried—and we are still trying! Painful as it is to admit it, Haiti is poorer today than it was then!

So why do it? Would it have been better if we had stayed home?

In her book *Words of Wisdom for the World,* Susan Muto gives new life to the Precautions of the Counsels of St. John of the Cross, written in the 16th century and said to be "the most detailed and concrete and practical set of rules for arriving at spiritual perfection ever seen." After warning us not to get absorbed in our work to the exclusion of God, she observes that, "The satisfaction or dissatisfaction we receive from doing a work is not the reason we do it. Our motive is freer than that. Agreeable or not, we do what we must for the sole motive of pleasing God."

Thank you, loving Lord, for granting us a place in your kingdom. Forgive us when we want to show impressive results, when we gloat over our accomplishments and grovel in our disappointments, forgetting that all things are from you, through you, and to you. Grant that we may be worthy servants, wanting above all to please you and give you the glory. Amen.

— **Edgar Stoesz, Akron, Pennsylvania**

Servanthood

"Then the mother of the sons of Zebedee . . . said to him, 'Command that these two sons of mine may sit, one at your right hand and one at your left, in your kingdom.' But Jesus answered, 'You do not know what you are asking . . . You know that the rulers of the Gentiles lord it over them . . . It shall not be so among you; but whoever would be great among you must be your servant . . . even as the Son of man came not to be served but to serve, and to give his life as a ransom for many.'"

— Matthew 20:20-22, 25-28 (RSV)

We had attended church together in a village in north India. The building was four walls, one door, and, as I remember, one window. The floor was dirt. There were neither benches nor chairs. A mixed crowd of maybe 80 people came to worship that Sunday.

After the simple but meaningful service, we left immediately in a well-worn VW micro-bus. Quickly, spontaneously, the Hindi-speaking Indians clustered in the front; the English speakers in the rear. Both groups were involved in animated discussion above the rattles and rumbles of the engine. Suddenly the Indians laughed uproariously. We were curious.

Anil related a dream. For many years he had been the house servant of the respected Mennonite mission leader, Joe Graber. In this dream Anil had died and found himself in heaven, seated at the head of the table, being served by his former master. That seemed very strange to him and his friends and was the cause of their laughter.

We tried to enjoy the dream with the Indians, but it obviously had a deeper meaning for them. Finally someone asked Anil which role he had enjoyed more, servant or master? His instant reply was, "Oh, servant of course!"

Is it so for us? Our culture expects us to aspire to positions of power and prominence. Proudly we accept the congratulations of our friends or sit at the head of the table. Eagerly we look for our pictures in the paper. How easy it is for us to do the right thing for the wrong reasons.

As I reflect on my church service career, including a variety of administrative and board roles, the most truly enjoyable, the most satisfying by far, were those which permitted me to render service directly to persons in need. Positions of high visibility are, at worst, like mined fields; at best they are impersonal and remote. Few things are so deeply satisfying as giving a cup of cold water in the master's name.

We ask simply, Lord, give us the hearts of servants, seeking not to be served, not to lord it over others, but to serve. Teach us that it is in giving that we receive; it is in dying to self that we are ushered into a more meaningful life. Even as you girded yourself with the towel and washed the feet of the disciples, so grant that we may serve each other and, in so doing, serve you. Amen.

It is more blessed to give than to receive.

— Edgar Stoesz, Akron, Pennsylvania

Blessed
Are the Poor
in Spirit

"And he sat . . . and watched the multitude putting money into the treasury. Many rich people put in large sums. And a poor widow came, and put in two copper coins . . . And he called his disciples to him, and said to them, 'Truly, I say to you, this poor widow has put in more than all those who are contributing to the treasury. For they all contributed out of their abundance; but she out of her poverty has put in everything she had, her whole living.'"

— Mark 12:41-44 (RSV)

They were sitting on the floor of the Sumanahalli Leprosy Centre near Bangalore, India, mabe eight or 10 of them, working. Some were stringing beads; others were re-rolling yarn. Leprosy had rendered them disfigured, outcasts. Fingers or toes were missing, sometimes an entire hand or foot, leaving these persons severely disabled. Several were blind. Beggars, they had been gathered from the streets.

We greeted them and continued our tour. Moments later our guide was interrupted by a messenger. After a whispered conversation we were asked if we would return. One of them, it seemed, wanted to sing for us. We went back.

Veera Muthu greeted us with a happy, almost toothless, smile. His both legs had been amputated; one at the ankle, the other below the knee. One hand had a thumb, the other a finger. His nose was disfigured, but his delight was apparent. He sang with a clear, melodious, natural voice, accompanied with his homemade tambourine which he held in one hand, thumping it against the stump of the other.

The words were in Tamil. I was lost in thought, but then . . . was I hearing correctly? Yes, "A Happy New Year." Another verse and again, "A Happy New Year." Later I was told he had sung us a blessing, asking Jesus to dispel the darkness and send the light. We were touched.

Veera had managed somehow to accommodate himself to his harsh reality. Within that twisted body, under those tattered clothes, resided a beautiful spirit. Through him the darkness was dispelled and the light of Jesus shone on us, however briefly.

Forgive us, loving Lord, when we complain about what we don't have, when we overlook the rich blessings we enjoy, when we complain about not having enough shoes while others have no feet. Forgive us for thinking that what we have is too small to make a difference. Teach us to bring what we have and are and to put that on the altar for you to bless and use and extend your kingdom. Amen.

Veera had two fingers; he had no toes or feet. He did have a song in his heart for people with 10 fingers and 10 toes, but who were without a song.

— Edgar Stoesz, Akron, Pennsylvania

We Find God
in the Poor

"Woe to him who builds his house by unrighteousness . . . who says, 'I will build myself a great house with spacious upper rooms,' and cuts out windows for it, paneling it with cedar, and painting it with vermilion. Do you think you are a king because you compete in cedar? Did not your father eat and drink and do justice and righteousness? Then it was well with him. He judged the cause of the poor and needy; then it was well. Is not this to know me? says the Lord."

— Jeremiah 22:13-16 (RSV)

I almost stopped reading to ease my distress. An article in the church magazine carried the title, "Putting your church's money where its mission statement is." It had this to say: "I've never read a mission statement that says we want to be a self-serving church, focusing only on our own needs and ignoring the needs of those around us. Yet a church that would never think of saying this in its mission statement often says something very close to it in another document that probably reveals more than any other about its real priorities—the budget."

I really felt pushed to the edge when I read, "Most churches today spend less than three percent of their income on the needy within the congregation and the surrounding community—a far cry from the 50 percent advocated by Calvin, and the even higher percentage practiced by the New Testament church. Is it any wonder that so many non-Christians view today's church as one more self-serving institution . . . ?"

I once had a dream in which God showed me that God must be found in the face of the poor. Actually, it was probably a vision rather than a dream. I was on a five-day prayer and writing retreat. It was the middle of the night and my soul hungered for God. I rolled over and turned on the radio. What did I expect? I don't know. But in the darkness came a singing voice, "The words of the prophets are written on the subway walls and tenement halls." This said to me, that's where you will hear from God. You will see God where the poor express themselves.

Oh God, whose heart is filled with compassion for the poor, lead me and the organizations to which I belong to the poor. There let us find you, as you have promised. Amen.

"The poor give us more than we give them. They're such strong people, living day-to-day without food. And they never curse, never complain. We don't have to give them pity or sympathy. We have so much to learn from them."—Mother Teresa (1977)

— John K. Stoner, Akron, Pennsylvania

Keep Breathing

"Then the Lord God formed man from the dust of the ground and breathed into his nostrils the breath of life, and the man became a living being."

— Genesis 2:7 (NRSV)

"The Spirit of God has made me, and the breath of the Almighty gives me life."

— Job 33:4 (NRSV)

"And with that he breathed on them and said, 'Receive the Holy Sprit.'"

— John 20:22 (NIV)

The most important rule in scuba diving is, "Keep breathing. Never hold your breath." Divers must overcome their natural instinct to hold their breaths under water. It's a matter of life and death. If divers hold their breaths, the expansion of the compressed air they breathe can rupture their lung sacs and cause death.

Even experienced divers can have moments when they are tempted to hold their breaths. Imagine swimming deep underwater in a clear blue sea. Suddenly you are confronted by an underwater creature that is larger than you. Or imagine swimming over the edge of a beautiful coral reef to find yourself staring into a huge, bottomless abyss. When surprised or scared, we naturally react with an inhaled gasp that we can hardly let go.

We often respond the same way when we face an organizational crisis or setback. If revenues fall or unexpected expenses soar or staff fail or leave, we can be so stunned that we are almost paralyzed. We can become so obsessed with the problem that we lose sight of our organizational goals and mission. We become knee-jerk reactive instead of creatively responsive.

As it is for scuba divers, the secret to our succeeding is often as simple as "Just keep breathing." Divers are acutely aware of their breathing. The sound of air flowing through the regulator is often the only sound one hears while swimming underwater. For just a moment or two now, concentrate on your breathing. Listen to it; feel it. It is a powerful force.

As we breathe, we can become co-creators with God. We can breathe life into our organizations and projects by breathing life into the solutions that will resolve a crisis or difficulty. As we breathe, creativity flows. As we breathe, we draw closer to God.

Breathe on us, breath of God. Fill us with life anew. As we face our need, help us remember your life-giving breath. Grant us the courage to join you in breathing life into this organization so its mission and ministry may continue to serve you. Amen.

The breath of God dwells in each of us. It is the Holy Spirit.

— Carol Suter, Kansas City, Missouri

Feeding the Hand that Bites You

"But I tell you who hear me: Love your enemies, do good to those who hate you, bless those who curse you, pray for those who mistreat you. If someone strikes you on one cheek, turn to him the other also. If someone takes your cloak, do not stop him from taking your tunic. Give to everyone who asks you, and if anyone takes what belongs to you, do not demand it back. But love your enemies, do good to them, and lend to them without expecting to get anything back . . . Then you will be sons of the Most High, because he is kind to the ungrateful and wicked."

— Luke 6:27-35 (NIV)

William Sloane Coffin, the great Protestant preacher, tells the story of a man trying to free a scorpion tangled and entrapped in the roots of a mangrove tree. Every time the old man gets near, the scorpion stings him. The old man does not relent in his effort to aid. The scorpion does not relent in its stinging. After several attempts, the old man gives up, his hand so swollen that he cannot manipulate his fingers. A cynical bystander ridicules the old man as a fool. The man replies, "Just because the scorpion's nature is to sting, doesn't change my nature which is to save."

Disappointment in and rejection by those we are trying to help can be devastating even to the strongest and most well-intentioned Christian. This devastation is understandable from a human standpoint, but it is not justifiable from a biblical standpoint. As Jesus tells us in the Sermon on the Mount, we can expect rejection, we can expect disappointment, we can even expect hostility. The way to destruction is wide, broad, and smooth. The way to eternal life is narrow, rocky, and difficult. The Bible is about faith and righteousness, not effectiveness and results.

Clarence Jordan exhibited faithfulness when he developed Koinonia Farm, an experiment in communal Christian living in southwest Georgia. The Farm was founded on the principles of Christian peacemaking, simple living, and economic equality. These were very controversial concepts in the post-war period. As a result of putting his faith into practice, Jordan and his humble little fellowship were boycotted, beaten up, shot at, and dynamited. This opposition drove many of its members away, causing a reporter to ask Jordan if he thought he was successful. Jordan replied, "I reckon about as successful as the crucifixion."

We are not called to squash or even avoid the scorpions of our time, but to save them. We are not promised a life of pleasure, free of pain and suffering. We are called to be open to the truth of the crucifixion. We are called to be faithful, not successful. This is not bad, depressing news. This is the good news of the Gospel for, as Jesus promised, "in losing our life, we find it."

Lord help us to be faithful to your word, not to conform to our world. Open us to the powerful truth of the life of Jesus as he gave himself to save us. Energize us so that we can reach out to those in need. Strengthen us to love unconditionally. Amen.

God, go behind us as our strength, go beside us as our friend, go beneath us as our support, go ahead of us as our guide, and go above us as our light.

—Ted Swisher, Americus, Georgia

Mountains of Privilege, Valleys of Need

*"The voice of one crying out in the wilderness,
'Prepare the way of the Lord, make his paths straight.
Every valley shall be filled, and every mountain and
hill shall be made low . . .Whoever has two coats
must share with anyone who has none; and whoever
has food must do likewise.'"*

— Luke 3:4-5a, 11 (NRSV)

While driving in the mountains of east Kentucky, I came upon an interesting cross-section of road-building history. Just over the shoulder of the modern highway and down a little incline were the remains of another road from perhaps the middle of the century. Then beyond the shoulder of that road and down another little incline was yet a third road that likely dated from the early part of the century. It took no genius to deduct from this cross-section that improvement in road-building meant building roads wider, straighter, and smoother as new technology permitted.

That is also the point in this passage from Luke. Based upon Isaiah's prophecy (Isaiah 40:4-5), John the Baptist is ministering by preparing the way for the Lord and his coming kingdom. The essence of this preparation is to "make his paths straight," leveling out the rough places by filling up the valleys and bringing down the mountains.

Of course, what is being leveled here is not the physical terrain. Instead, it is about the inequities and differences among people. It speaks of the valleys of need and the mountains of privilege. It sees a correlation between the heights of the mountains and the depths of the valleys. The only way the valleys of need can be filled is by sharing some of the privilege that has made the mountains so high.

When John was asked what his message of repentance meant *practically*, he applied it economically and talked about food and clothes. He said, in effect, that when someone lives on the mountain of two coats and someone else lives in the valley of no coats, the one who lives on the mountain should give the coat he isn't wearing to the man who lives in the valley. Then they can live comfortably together on the level plane of one coat.

Dear God, thank you for the abundance of your blessings. Help us with the mountains of privilege we possess to find opportunities for sharing our ample resources with others. Amen.

— W. Clyde Tilley, Seymour, Tennessee

How Much
Is Enough?

*"I'll tear down my barns and build bigger ones! I will
have room enough."*

— Luke 12:18 (TLB)

How much is enough? How many barns, how much land,
how many dollars, how many homes, how many automobiles, how many clothes, does one person need?
How does one know when one has enough? When does the
moment come when the soul says to the mind, that is *enough*,
you have plenty! Stop accumulating!

Dan West, founder of Heifer Project International, observed
that, "It is difficult to be content with little, but it is impossible
to be content with much."

Jesus talked about a farmer who was not content with his
much. He wanted bigger barns in which to store his more-than-
needed wealth, and all at the expense of his soul. John Moiré,
environmentalist and writer early in this century, was talking
with a friend about a very wealthy railroad magnate of that day.
"He is so extremely wealthy," the friend said to Moiré.

"But I am more wealthy," said John.

"What do you mean?" exclaimed the friend. "You scarcely
have a penny to your name."

"But I have all I want," said Moiré, "and that railroad man
does not. I am more wealthy than he."

In a *Christianity Today* article Joe Catkins writes about
"feeding the monster called more." His article is basically
about gambling, but it focuses exactly on what Jesus and Dan
West were talking about—the propensity in human nature for

wanting more than one has, at the expense of the needs of others.

If our world is to survive with any kind of justice and compassion, multiplied millions of us who are affluent must learn when "enough is enough," and we must begin to share with others to a far greater degree. Mother Teresa said that "if we only give away that which we do not need, we do nothing."

Almighty Creator, who owns the earth and all in it and whom we claim as our God, help us to fathom within our minds when we have our share of earth's bounties. Stay our hand from grabbing more. Open our eyes to the needs of others, our ears to their cries for relief, and then our hearts and hands to share with them. We pray in the name of the one who gave all. Amen.

There is so little we really need to live a happy and fulfilled life.
—Elaine S. James

— Mel West, Columbia, Missouri

A House
of Four Rooms

"And thou shalt love the Lord thy God with all thy
heart, and with all thy soul, and with all thy mind and
with all thy strength; this is the first commandment."
— Mark 12:30 (KJV)

"There is an Indian belief," according to Rumer Godden, "that everyone is a house of four rooms: a physical, a mental, an emotional, and a spiritual room. Most of us tend to live in one room most of the time, but unless we go into every room every day, even if only to keep it aired, we are not complete."

Jesus went further than that in his statement. We are to visit each of those four rooms daily and experience them in all their fullness.

We are each to experience and love God with the full power of the amazing physical body which we have each been given, treasuring and maintaining it for long service. We are each to experience and love God with the full power of the magnificent mind placed within that body, the gift of our own personal computer. We are each to experience and love God with the full power of the emotional being of feeling which we each are. And we are each to experience and love God with the full power of the unique spirit, that soul, which inhabits and tunes each of us into the divine spark.

Jesus seems to be saying, full power ahead, pedal to the metal, with all that we have and are. No holds barred. Give it all you have. And, indeed, he seemed to live such a life. Is it possible for us to do so?

If we fail as individuals, for we do tend to "live in one room most of the time," we can perhaps live more perfectly as a group. Some are much more "feeling" persons than others, and the group needs that alertness at times. Speak out. Some are more spiritually inclined. Keep close to the universe and to us. Some are more action-oriented. We need you. And some have long-proven intellectual gifts of wisdom that seem to come from beyond. Share that with us.

Divine Creator, we do not want to die having only half lived. Enable us to visit daily every room in the house which is us and to meet you there in the passing. Amen.

Leave the doors ajar; it will be easier to return.

— Mel West, Columbia, Missouri

To the Least
of These

"And the King will answer them, 'Truly, I say to you,
as you did it to one of the least of these my brethren,
you did it to me.'"

— Matthew 25:40 (RSV)

The scripture is simple, direct, and profound. It is a picture of the Last Judgment. The judge, God, will separate those who come before the throne. The test is really rather simple—what have you done for the poor, the handicapped, the neglected and rejected, the marginalized, the imprisoned, the "least" persons you can imagine? Those who have responded favorably to the needs of such persons can expect a favorable reward. Those who did not cannot.

Perhaps a country should be judged not by the size of its armies, its scientific achievements, or its universities, but by the way it ministers to its children, its elderly, its sick, and its imprisoned. There are simple models around to observe, if we choose to look. Each Sunday morning at 9:30 in a church in Columbia, Missouri, a young woman named Cindy is the acolyte. She has performed that same task proudly and well for a number of years. She is a most beloved member and servant of that congregation. She has Down's syndrome. As one of the "least of these" she has found her place in that church.

The popular TV program "L.A. Law" featured a mentally disabled young man who served in the role of messenger and office attendant. Some fast-food chains employ persons who are intellectually challenged.

Is it possible that our businesses, our programs, our projects, our organizations, will ultimately be judged not by how high the salaries of the executives were, nor by how brilliant the staff was, but rather by how respectfully and effectively those persons whom Jesus called "the least" were woven into the organizations' structures and programs?

Almighty God, Father and Mother of us all, you who call us into one family, encourage and enable us to seek out those sisters and brothers who need love and attention the most and to begin with them. Help us to raise our standards of achievement to those exemplified by Jesus, our Lord. Amen.

Ponder how the bottom lines of *The Wall Street Journal* and Matthew 25 differ. Are they at all compatible?

— Mel West, Columbia, Missouri

How Many Work
in Your Shop?

*"The earth is the Lord's, and the fulness thereof; the
world, and they that dwell therein."*

— Psalm 24:18a (KJV)

While studying in a language school in San Jose, Costa
Rica, I developed the habit of taking walks each after-
noon. The brilliant green rows of coffee were con-
toured lovingly around the rolling hills. Irrigation ditches trick-
led along the roadside, and the native birds serenaded me at
each turn. It was a welcome respite from the classroom and an
opportunity to practice Spanish with local persons.

A roadside shop caught my attention. It was perhaps 10 feet
wide and 40 feet long, made of crude lumber and tin, a lean-to
against a larger building. As I stepped inside I saw wooden bed-
steads for sale. They were hand-carved, and a bit crude, but
sturdy and with a unique air of elegance.

The carpenter came to the front, and I explained to him that
I was not there to buy, but was interested in him and what he
was doing. This brought forth a tour of the shop. He used rough
lumber and smoothed it by hand. His tools were simple and the
work labor-intensive. With great pride he showed me a corner
shelf he was making.

I asked how many people worked in the shop. He replied
"*Dos*" (two). I looked around for the other person. He smiled
and pointed to himself and said, "*Uno,*" then pointed toward
the heavens and said, "*Y Dios.*" He and God worked in the
shop. Reaching for a piece of rough lumber, he explained to me
that God made the trees, and that he made the beds. Pointing

to a finished bed frame he said, *"Dios y Yo"* (God and I).

His theology was simple and yet profound. As I walked on I reflected upon how those of us who came from the farm knew we were dependent on the forces of God's created order—rain, the sun, the land. How many persons today consider God to be a full partner in their work or business? Such an attitude would lead us to comments like, "God made the ore; we make the automobiles." "God laid down the laws of physics; we make the computer chips." "God created that child, and I help prepare him/her for life."

Divine Creator, help us to realize that we are your full partners. You gave us life and you receive us in death. Everything we touch is of your creation. May we daily breathe the prayer, "Dios y Yo." God and I. Amen.

The shadow of God is always with you if you walk in the Light.

— Mel West, Columbia, Missouri

Called to
Super-Vision

"Where there is no vision, the people perish."

— Proverbs 29:18a (KJV)

God grants the capacity to have vision to all who seek God's Spirit. Joel 2:28 says that when "God pours out the Spirit," all will have visions and dreams about the potential for the Kingdom—young and old, rich and poor, male and female, slave and master. Even the most humble person is granted the gift of visioning and dreaming.

But some are called to that unusually responsible task of "super-vision," named to be "super-visors" for an organization. The name immediately implies something beyond the routine. The call is not to extra-ordinary rewards, although rewards there are, but to extra-ordinary responsibilities.

We are called to have super-vision in regards to the goals for this organization. What are our mission and purpose? What is God calling us to do at this time in history?

We are called to have super-vision into our past and to learn from it. What rearview-mirror lessons should we learn from our past? We do not automatically learn from our mistakes.

We are called to have super-vision about the impact of our actions. Every decision we make will have implications that are social, environmental, cultural, political, and economic. Everything we touch will shake something else. Our actions do indeed call for super-vision.

We are called to have super-vision into the minds and souls of those with whom we work. As persons in positions of authority, we often do not realize how our every word, comment, and decision affect the persons over which we have super-vision. One thoughtless act or word from us can shatter their lives.

We are called to have super-vision in the future. What directions are emerging and how will they affect our mission? We are the "scouts" for the organization—looking for the vision from the high spot. The entire wagon-train of the organization will follow us wherever we lead—to destruction or to the promised land.

God, we do not feel super-ior, but we do know we are called to tasks demanding super-vision. We have far too big a task without help from an outside power. We call upon you for that. Walk with us . . . empower us . . . be our first and major consultant. In the name of Jesus we ask it, Amen.

To become an adequate super-visor, one also needs super-humility, super-love, super-patience, super-endurance, super-faith, and super-kindness.

— Mel West, Columbia, Missouri

Running Low
on Spiritual Fuel

"Do not be deceived; God is not mocked, for you reap whatever you sow. If you sow to your own flesh, you will reap corruption from the flesh; but if you sow to the Spirit, you will reap eternal life from the Spirit. So let us not grow weary in doing what is right, for we will reap at harvest time, if we do not give up. So then, whenever we have an opportunity, let us work for the good of all."

— Galatians 6:7-10a (NRSV)

I was en route to the airport on a 10-lane beltway in a large eastern city. The traffic was gridlocked, bumper to bumper with little forward progress. I was in the middle of five lanes. The airport was still 22 miles ahead when a beeper went off in my car. Looking to the instrument panel I saw the low-fuel light was on.

A range of emotions went through me. At first I simply stared in disbelief. Soon, however, I panicked, realizing the fix I was in. Then I became angry. First I was angry at myself, wondering how I could let such a thing happen. Soon I directed my anger away from myself towards others. I began blaming "them" for my predicament. If only the church I was visiting hadn't kept me so long, I would have remembered to fuel up before leaving. If that one person hadn't talked about so many details . . . My empty fuel tank temporarily paralyzed my ability to think rationally.

I find that these same emotions affect many of us when our spiritual fuel tanks are nearly empty. We become panicky, blaming, angry persons, quick to move responsibility away from our-selves.

Our first order of business as boards and management is to ensure that our spiritual tanks have plenty of fuel. We must give adequate attention to the cultivation of our inner lives. Only then can we face the challenges of our work and do it with steadiness and vision. Our spiritual fitness provides the frame-work and foundation for the wisdom we need to meet the ser-vice and product needs of our world.

Gracious God, help us see the limitations and the futility of run-ning on empty. Help us understand that prayer and meditation belong at the top of our daily "to do" lists. Create in us an awareness and hunger for being in daily communion with you. Fill our spiritual tanks with the fuel of your Holy Spirit, that we might make decisions and plans that please you and bring love and service to our communities. Amen.

Our first order of business is to keep our spiritual tanks filled.

— David Wine, Abilene, Kansas

From Where Does
My Help Come?

"I lift up my eyes to the hills—from where will my help come? My help comes from the Lord who made heaven and earth. He will not let your foot be moved; he who keeps you will not slumber, he who keeps Israel will neither slumber nor sleep. The Lord is your keeper; the Lord is your shade at your right hand. The sun shall not strike you by day, nor the moon by night. The Lord will keep you from all evil; he will keep your life. The Lord will keep your going out and your coming in from this time on and forevermore."

— Psalm 121 (NRSV)

I had the opportunity to teach at Union Biblical Seminary in Pune, India. I enjoyed comparing UBS's different style and setting—and tea breaks—with campus life at the seminary where I usually taught. The cultural differences were educational, but I was not prepared for the difference in faculty meetings. In the U.S. our faculty meetings always opened with a "paragraph" of prayer before we got on to the real work of the meeting. But not so at the UBS faculty meetings. In India we began with a devotional that often turned into a Bible study or a sermon. That was followed by a time of robust prayer that often turned into an old-fashioned prayer meeting—with all attending sharing their concerns for the church, for the school, for their students and their colleagues, and then fervently praying for the expressed needs. After tea we regrouped to spend a few minutes doing the faculty's business.

I'm not suggesting that all meetings should be run this way.

What has given me pause, however, is the question, where does my help come from? Who is the source of my strength and wisdom? My brothers and sisters in India seemed to understand that their help and strength and wisdom came from the Lord and not from their own cleverness, not from their creativity with numbers or program, not from the introduction of a new product. Their help came from the Lord.

Oh Lord, our God, Creator of the Universe!
We look to you at the beginning of this meeting to ask you
    to be our help,
    to be our strength, and
    to be our wisdom.
Forgive us when we make idols of our own cleverness
    and creativity.
Forgive us when we fail to remember that all we have and know
    is a gift from you.
We offer to you the work of today and ask you
    to bless us,
    to bless our time together,
    and to remind us that we are your creation.
In the name of Jesus we pray, Amen.

My help comes from the Lord who made heaven and earth.

— **June Alliman Yoder, Elkhart, Indiana**

What a Waste of Resources!

"While Jesus was at Bethany in the house of Simon the leper, sitting at the table, a woman came with an alabaster jar of very costly ointment of nard. She broke open the jar and poured the ointment on his head. But some were there who said to one another in anger, 'Why was the ointment wasted in this way? For this ointment could have been sold for more than three hundred denarii, and the money given to the poor.' And they scolded her. But Jesus said, 'Let her alone; why do you trouble her? She has performed a good service for me. For you always have the poor with you and you can show kindness to them whenever you wish; but you will not always have me. She has done what she could; she has anointed my body beforehand for its burial. Truly I tell you, wherever the good news is proclaimed in the whole world, what she has done will be told in remembrance of her.'"

— Mark 14:3-9 (NRSV)

A denomination was experiencing a major conflict in its worldwide church body over a significant issue of orthodoxy. And thus it was that a consultation was planned, and each country was invited to send a delegation to discuss the issue. The time for the meeting arrived, and among all the delegates were three people representing the church in Cuba.

The meeting progressed fairly smoothly and the time of adjournment drew near. It was only as people were bidding one another farewell that they began to realize that only two of the three people from Cuba had spoken. Everyone else had participated. They had spent hard-earned money to get to this meeting. You wouldn't do that and then not have something to say. Why had the church in Cuba sent three delegates and why did the third person say nothing? What a huge waste of the church's resources!

Only then did the Cuban delegates speak up. "We brought the third person to pray. His job was to pray for the consultation, for us, and for the church. His contribution was great, and he wasn't a waste."

Think about our meetings. Some of them deal with very weighty issues that affect the lives of many people and their families. We hire and fire, we eliminate positions and transfer people, we close offices and whole factories. Perhaps it would not be a waste to designate a person to be in prayer for our deliberations.

O God, we are aware that you can be honored by holy waste. Forgive us for being too cost-conscious when it comes to demonstrating our love for you. Forgive us for being too thrifty when it comes to demonstrating our trust in you. Forgive us for allowing stingy economic principles to dictate what should be dictated by your principles of compassion. O God, we desire you to be present in our deliberations today. Fill your hearts with generosity motivated by your love for us. In the name of Jesus we pray, Amen.

Sometimes "waste" is a good investment.

— June Alliman Yoder, Elkhart, Indiana

Prayers

The following prayers are all by James David Ford, Chaplain of the United States House of Representatives. The prayers acknowledge the work of God—and the work of a group of people, joined in a common task.

Do Not Forget Us

From the first hours of new life to the last rays of the sun, from the opening of each day of grace to the final moments of our time, may we, O gracious God, not neglect our words of prayer, praise, and thanksgiving. While we know how easily we are absorbed in our tasks and our eyes miss the heavenly vision, we know, too, that you do not forget us. We acknowledge that our lives stray here or there, yet we know, too, that your goodness and your love sustain us all our days. For these and all your blessings, O God, we offer these words of thanksgiving.

Amen.

Show Us the Way

O God our help in ages past, our hope for years to come, we come before you in this quiet moment of prayer with our petitions both great and small. We place before you our aspirations and hopes, our dreams and our ambitions, asking that you bless that which is good and honorable and show us the way of truth.

May your spirit correct us when wrong, amend our willful deeds, and teach us the power of faith and hope and love in all we do or ask or say. In your name, we pray.

Amen.

Transform Us

O gracious God, from whom comes every good and perfect gift, we offer our thanks for this day and for new opportunities. As we open our hearts to your grace and heed your Word, may we be transformed by the renewing of our minds and spirits, so all that which hinders or hurts is put aside and that which redeems and reforms and forgives remains with each of us.

With gratitude and praise we offer these words of prayer, together with the private petitions of our hearts, asking you to bless us and keep us the rest of this day and all the days long.

Amen.

May We Act Mercifully

As our hearts are full of the blessings of this life and abounding in gratitude for opportunities for service, we pause in this our prayer, O God, to ask for that spiritual strength and compass that you alone can give. Point us to the way of justice, direct us with the vision of mercy, sustain us with your abiding presence, and encourage us always to celebrate and sustain our rich heritage. For all these tasks which can seem so daunting, we pray for your blessing and your peace.

Amen.

We are Thankful; Keep Us Faithful

For the sun to brighten the day, for the rains to nurture the land, for challenges to be confronted and responsibilities to be accepted, for sacrifices to be endured and for all of life to be fully lived, for friends to accompany and for family to love, we offer these words, O God, of thanksgiving and praise.

We earnestly pray that we will be faithful to the opportunities and the tasks that are before us, so that in all things, we will do your will and serve people according to their need.

Amen.

Help Us to See Clearly

We pray, gracious God, for a clear vision of ourselves and of the world in which we live and work and have our being. Enable us to see ourselves as we truly are—created in your image and marked by opportunities to be the people you would have us be—and make us also aware that we often miss the mark and lose the vision. We know, O God, that if we do not see the heavenly vision and miss the direction for our lives, our steps will wander and we will lose our way.

Open our eyes, gracious God, so we see the path to freedom and opportunity and of service to others. This is our earnest prayer.

Amen.

We Are Blessed

As the psalmist of old has written: I will call to mind the deeds of the Lord; yea, I will remember thy wonders of old. I will meditate on all thy work, and muse on thy mighty deeds (Psalm 77: 11-12).

In our best seasons, O God, we realize the marvelous moments of your whole creation—the wonders of the universe, the majesty of life, the magnificence of human opportunity, the gifts of faith and hope and love. Remind us this day, O God, that in addition to that which is before us and is to be accomplished, we pause in prayer to give thanks to you for your mighty deeds to us and to all people and to express our gratitude for all the blessings of life and love. This is our earnest prayer.

Amen.

Which Way to Justice and Mercy?

As your Word tells us to do justly and to love mercy, help us, O God, to walk the path of justice and mercy in our lives. We admit that our ways are weak and our wishes can miss the mark and we too easily mind our own way. We know, too, that there are many paths available to us and there are choices we make every day.

We pray, gracious God, for the insight and wisdom to follow the path that leads to faith, the road that strengthens hope, and the way that celebrates love. This is our earnest prayer.

Amen.

Give Us Understanding

Encourage each person, O loving God, to examine the issues that each encounters and on which each must act, and to have discernment as each faces the decisions of the time. Help us to be forthright in our desire for knowledge, realizing that the gift of truth is not to be scorned, but with virtuous hearts and sincere minds we should seek to understand the issues of life. Help us to endeavor, in all things, to remember the words of the Proverbs that "the fear of the Lord is the beginning of wisdom, and the knowledge of the Holy One is insight."

Amen.

May We Live Up to Our Calling

For all the opportunities, O God, that lie before us and every person, we offer our thanks; for all the possibilities for knowledge and understanding, we are grateful; for friends and family and colleagues who support us and help show the way, we express our gratitude. May we be so fervent in our tasks, gracious God, that we will be worthy of the calling we have been given, to be of service to other people in doing the deeds of justice and by providing leadership in the cause of peace and reconciliation for every person. Bless us this day and every day, we pray.

Amen.

Give Us the Right Words

Teach us always, gracious God, to use our words as instruments of information and understanding, as agents of communication and contact, so that our expressions bring us together and allow us to share in our common heritage and our collective concerns.

Remind us that we should choose our words wisely, for we know that comments clearly stated and given for the purpose of knowledge can promote harmony and mutual assurance and can lead all people to greater respect and reverence toward one another. Bless us and all your people, O God, this day and every day.

Amen.

We Ask for Your Light

We are reminded by the Psalmist that your Word, O God, is a lamp to our feet and a light to our path. In these times when there are many options available to people in their lives, and diverse opinions and ideas, we pray for lamps to lighten our way and show us the course to follow.

We recognize that we can communicate with great authority from many backgrounds and attempt to gain all knowledge, and yet we know that to be touched by your spirit is the beginning of wisdom. May that spirit, O God, that is new every morning, encourage and lighten our path, now and evermore.

Amen.

We Need Your Strength

O gracious God, to whom we address our prayers and petitions and from whom comes every good gift, we pray for the strength of mind and body and spirit so that we will do the works of justice and mercy. As the prophet Isaiah has reminded us, we can grow weary and tired in our labors. Yet we are comforted by the prophet's words that they who wait upon the Lord shall renew their strength, they shall mount up with wings like eagles, they shall run and not be weary. We pray for your strength, O God, that sustains in all the seasons of our lives, so we will do your good work this day and every day.

Amen.

We Want to Be Your People

With the words of the Psalmist we pray that you would search us, O God, and know our hearts, try us and know our thoughts, and see if there be any wicked way in us, and lead us in the way everlasting. We pray, almighty God, that through reflection and meditation, through study and edification, and above all through prayer and renewed faith, we will speak with truth, our minds will point to justice, and our hearts will be full of mercy, that in all things, you will be our God and we will be your people. Bless us now in all we do, and may your spirit remain with us always.

Amen.

May We Insist on Adequate Quietness

We pray, O God, that in the business of every day, we will use our time wisely so we will gain healthy and holy lives. Remind us that our value comes not only in action in the cluttered hours of work, but also in reflection and meditation and prayer and an awareness of your abiding spirit in our lives.

As we take some time for those precious moments and quiet deliberation and circumspection, may we grow in the assurance that your power and your peace are sufficient for our needs.

Amen.

Prompt Us to Express Gratitude

Teach us, O gracious God, to be responsive to the prayers and blessings and support that other people share with us. When we truly examine our lives, we see how those about us have favored us with both material and spiritual gifts, and we too often only accept the gift and never offer our appreciation to the giver.

Remind us always, O God, to be grateful for the support and advocacy of other people in our daily lives so we will respond with a true spirit of thanksgiving.

Amen.

We Are Caught in Complexities

We remember in this prayer, O gracious God, those who seek to serve people in their concerns and who endeavor to do your will. We pray also for all those who are burdened by the pressures and tensions of daily living and who struggle where values are weighed and who are immersed in the complexities and priorities of justice. As people face these concerns, we pray that they will be comforted by your presence and sustained by your good spirit, this day and every day.

Amen.

Connect What We Say with What We Do

We pray, O God, that our words of hope and our vision for justice will connect with our deeds, that our faith will be active in love, that all that we say with our lips, we will believe in our hearts, and all that we believe in our hearts we will practice in our daily lives.

Teach each person, O God, to relate words and deeds so we may have fidelity of character and sincerity of purpose in what we say and in what we do. This is our earnest prayer.

Amen.

Thank You for Rest

At the first moments of dawn we are reminded, O God, that your grace has come upon us, as free and as available as the morning sun. When the cool of the evening ends the day and the rush of business is hushed and the tumult of all life's concerns is at ease, we are reminded of the rest and the peace that your Word does give. For all these gifts and your daily blessings we offer this word of prayer and thanksgiving.

Amen.

We Need Others

Our hearts are grateful, O loving God, that we are surrounded by others who support us in our worries, who celebrate with us in our victories, and whose presence is ever with us. At our best moments we acknowledge that we do not walk alone or possess all the strengths or energy or courage to face the opportunities and the challenges of each day.

With appreciation and with thanksgiving, we remember those whose lives are bound with ours and whose grace is ever with us. In your name we pray.

Amen.

Make Sense of Our Many Wishes

O gracious God, from whom we have come and to whom we belong, we place before you in this our prayer, our ambitions and our hopes, our dreams and our desires, asking that you bless that which is good and faithful and correct and amend what is selfish or unkind. We have so many plans for our lives and ideas for what ought to be. Yet many of our wishes are not accomplished and we feel discouraged.

May your good spirit, O God, that gives life to each new day, refresh us and inspire us to go forward, knowing that your power will bless us and make us whole. In your name, we pray.

Amen.

Keep Us from Wearing Out

We pray, O gracious God, that the opportunities of this day will inspire each of us to see more clearly the ways in which we can do the works of justice and mercy. While the tasks of righteousness seem so great, may your good spirit enlighten, encourage, and sustain us so that we will not grow weary in well-doing, but eagerly accept our responsibilities as good stewards of the resources of the Lord. In your name, we pray.

Amen.

We Give Thanks for Others

On this day we acknowledge those people who have made a difference in our lives, and we remember them with admiration and gratitude. We are thankful, O gracious God, that we do not have to walk the road of life alone or meet the challenges of our day by ourselves, but, rather, our lives are enhanced and made full by the support and blessing of those near and dear to us.

For families whose nurture to us is overwhelming, for colleagues who help point the way, and for friends whose affection and trust surround us, we offer these words of thanksgiving and appreciation. In your name, we pray.

Amen.

Bless Those Who Serve

We pray, gracious God, that wherever we are or whatever we do, your benediction will accompany us and your blessing shall ever be with us. We are especially appreciative this day of those who have served in this place and who have sought to use their abilities to do the work of justice for all people and have been diligent in service to the people of this community.

Amen.

Hear Our Prayers

Our voices cry out with the Psalmist of old when we pray:

Out of the depths I cry to thee, O Lord!

Lord hear my voice!

Let thy ears be attentive to the voice of my supplications!

In this our prayer, O God, we speak silently our supplications, our petitions, our requests, our aspirations, and our dreams. Regard our supplications with favor, our petitions and requests with support, and our aspirations and our dreams with grace. With gratefulness and praise, we implore your blessing this day and every day.

Amen.

We Need You, O God

As the rain nourishes the earth, so may your grace, O God, nourish us in the depths of our souls, our minds, and our hearts. We strive to learn and master new tasks. We absorb the facts and figures of today's world, and we have all the resources of the intellect of the generations.

Yet on this day we pray that we will heed the needs of our souls, strengthen our inner being in faith, preserve the hope and renewal of our hearts, and, by so doing, walk in love and trust with you, our God, for ever and ever.

Amen.

Give Us Tenderness and Resolve

Open our eyes, O God, so we have a better vision of your glory; guide our words so we speak good news; strengthen our hands so we do the works of justice and peace; and move our hearts to feel compassion toward every person.

For all these gifts and the blessings of life, we offer this prayer of thanksgiving.

Amen.

We Pray for Peace

There are times when it seems our world is filled with the demons of violence and chaos, and yet, O God, we pray for peace. The lives of some women and men and children are irrevocably lost. Instead of hope there is despair, and instead of respect and compassion there is contempt and disdain.

O gracious God, from whom we have come and to whom we shall return, encourage all people of good will to think and speak and act in ways that strengthen the human bond and make right the covenant of peace.

Amen.

We Bring Our Whole Selves

We are grateful, O God, that our prayers can express the essential emotions and ideas of the human spirit, that we are free to call upon you in all the moments of life—for better or worse, for richer or poorer, in sickness and in health. And so we call upon you this day from the secret places of our own hearts, asking that you would bless us when we need blessing and forgive us when we need forgiving.

Above all else, we pray for your presence in our lives day by day and for your spirit that nurtures us with the good graces of life.

Amen.

Give Us Your Vision

We pray for the gift of vision, O God, for we know that when there is no vision, individuals and families and institutions do not thrive. Just as the flower receives its nourishment from the sun and the soil, so the human spirit is nourished by a vision of your presence in our lives and the support we receive from your abiding care.

We pray, O gracious God, that whatever our concerns or whatever our needs or whatever our hopes and dreams, we may realize the strength and comfort that comes when we open our hearts to your love. This is our earnest prayer.

Amen.

May We Give Freely

Remind each person, O gracious God, of the blessedness of giving rather than receiving, of the exhilaration of service to others and the fulfillment that comes with contributions to noble causes, of the joy that comes when there is hope for the day and peace at the end.

As there is no other gift that so truly makes us human, we acknowledge you, O God, with the gifts of thankfulness and gratitude.

Amen.

Help Us to Live Respectfully

As we seek to carry on our responsibilities, remind us, gracious God, of the need for righteousness and respect for every person; as we pursue the path of justice, remind us of your gift of mercy; as we aspire to the gifts of liberty, remind us of the heavenly vision.

O creator of all the earth, O judge of nations and people, we pray that we will use the abilities that you have given us in ways that reflect your word. Teach us, O God, to be humble in our service and steadfast in our commitment. This is our earnest prayer.

Amen.

Heal Us; Make Us Strong

In the stillness of this moment, in the quiet of our prayer, we place before you, O God, that which is in our hearts and souls, those thoughts and ideas and feelings that make us what we are and direct us along life's way. We pray, gracious God, that you would refresh us and encourage us, that you would heal our hearts and make us strong, that you would forgive us when we miss the mark and give peace to every soul.

For the wonders of the world and the little miracles of every day, we offer these words of prayer and thanksgiving. In your name, we pray.

Amen.

Sustain Us

Our prayers reach out this day for all those whose lives know the anguish of separation from those they love or who experience the emptiness that comes when the meaning and purpose of life is dimmed. O gracious God, as you have given us your word of assurance and comfort that we ever belong to you and that your grace is sufficient for every need, so minister to all your people with your words of promise and peace and hope. This is our earnest prayer.

Amen.

We Have Received So Much

With all the tasks that need to be done and with the noise and clamor of the world about us, we bow our heads in this, our prayer, giving thanks for all the blessings we have received. O gracious God, from whom comes every good gift, we lift our voices in gratitude for those whose lives have made clearer to us the meaning of faith and hope and love. The gift of faith has empowered us to hear your good word and to trust in your grace. The gift of hope allows us to see beyond any present trouble and catch the vision of lives made whole and a world at peace. Your gift of love brings us to a fuller understanding of our humanity and makes each day come alive. For all these gifts, O God, we offer this prayer of thanksgiving and praise.

Amen.

Keep Us Accountable

May your word, O God, that brought the earth into being and sustains us along life's way not only comfort us, but examine and correct us in our vision, our motivations, and our purposes. We know that we are accountable to you for our lives and responsible to each other for our deeds, so we pray that we will see your mighty purposes for justice among us.

Sustain us, strengthen us, judge us, forgive us, and minister to us in the depths of our hearts. This is our earnest prayer.

Amen.

Keep Us Faithful; Keep Us Responsible

We are grateful, O God, that you have given to us the goals of justice and the designs of freedom. Remind us this day, gracious God, that it is our work to develop the strategies and the plans of achieving those goals, being aware of the prodding of your spirit.

We know that you have given to each of us the abilities to do good works, so we pray that we will be faithful in our tasks, responsible in our actions, and fervent in our desire to serve. We pray this together with the petitions of our own hearts.

Amen.

We Rest in Your Goodness

Your blessings, O God, are new every morning; your favor looks over us and gives us peace; your benediction speaks the words of forgiveness and new life; your everlasting arms give support and strength. Through illness and health, through hope and tears, through joy and sorrow, and in all the moments of each day, we are grateful, O God, for your gifts of faith and hope and love.

Amen.

May We Pray Properly!

The prophet Isaiah asked some very penetrating questions. The answers lead us to an attitude of profound prayer:

Who has measured the waters in the hollow of his hand, measured heaven with a span and calculated the dust of the earth in a measure? Weighed the mountains and the hills in a balance? Who has directed the spirit of the Lord, or as his counselor has taught him? With whom did he take counsel, and who instructed him, and taught him the path of justice? Who taught him knowledge, and showed him the way of understanding? (Isaiah 40:12-14)

Almighty God, these questions expose the shallowness of our understanding of prayer. So often we come to you in prayer as if it were our responsibility to brief you on world affairs or current national problems. Or we come to prayer with our shopping list of needs as if you did not know all about us. And then there are times we try to get you to bless our plans about which we never consulted you.

Father, you created prayer for us to be with you, to know you, to have our characters emulate your character, and, most of all, to be filled with your spirit. So we humble ourselves. Instead of telling you what to do, we open ourselves completely to receive your marching orders and to follow you. In the name of the one who taught us to pray, Not my will but yours be done.

Amen.

Heal Us

We pray, O God, for your gift of healing—healing of body, mind, and spirit. Our petitions are for estrangement to be replaced by reconciliation and alienation to be replaced by trust. We pray that your spirit will touch people's lives, that illness will be displaced by strength, and anxiety be overcome with confidence. We place these petitions before you, O God, that your power, that created the heavens and the earth and every living person, will live in our lives and nurture us along life's way. This is our earnest prayer.

Amen.

Strengthen Those in Crisis

We remember, O gracious God, those who need a special measure of your grace and protection. We recall the needs of those who do not benefit from the support and love of family and must find their own way through the uncertainties of life. We pray for those whose lives are disrupted and torn apart by the conflicts in our world, even as we support all those who work for reconciliation and peace.

We remember those whose days are filled with struggles for the basic essentials of life and for those who have little hope. Fill their lives, O God, with the fullness of your spirit that they may be blessed by your presence and receive new hope by your Word. This is our earnest prayer.

Amen.

Hear Us, We Ask

With praise and adoration, with thanksgiving and gratitude, we offer our prayers to you, O God, and place our petitions before you. We pray for our world and our nation, for our communities and the people of every background and tradition, for family and friends and for ourselves.

We place before you, gracious God, our needs that are both great and small, those supplications that we hold in the secret places of our own hearts, asking that you would forgive us where we are weak or selfish, and strengthen us to do those good works that do justice and mercy. In your name, we pray.

Amen.

Thank You for Meaningful Jobs

As we contemplate our lives and the lives of those people that we know, we realize how cluttered are the agendas of daily living and how hurried is the pace that each day brings. Yet, O gracious God, we are thankful that we have our vocations, our work, our responsibilities, and our tasks by which we can support ourselves and serve others in their need.

We remember in our prayer those who have no work and yet who wish to use the abilities that you have given in ways that support themselves and those they love. As you have called us to do the works of justice in our world, so may we be appreciative of the opportunities we have to do the works of justice in our lives. In your name, we pray.

Amen.

An Index to Themes
in the Meditations

About the Writers

Wilma Ann Bailey, Grantham, Pennsylvania; college professor.

Atlee Beechy, Goshen, Indiana; retired college professor.

Curt Bechler, North Newton, Kansas; college professor/administrator.

Lois Beck, Grantham, Pennsylvania; college professor.

Buck Blankenship, Charlotte, North Carolina; business executive.

John David Burton, Williamsville, New York; pastor.

J. Daryl Byler, Washington, D.C.; attorney/relief agency staff person.

Sylvia Shirk Charles, Goshen, Indiana; campus pastor.

Lee Delp, Lansdale, Pennsylvania; business executive.

Christopher J. Doyle, Greenville, South Carolina; mission agency executive.

Trevor Durstin, London, England; pastor/mission agency executive.

Peter J. Dyck, Scottdale, Pennsylvania; retired pastor/retired relief agency executive.

John Eby, Dillsburg, Pennsylvania; college professor/administrator.

Deborah Fast, Akron, Pennsylvania; writer.

Reta Halteman Finger, Harrisonburg, Virginia; college professor.

Gilbert E. Fleer, Columbia, Missouri; professor/pastor.

Ardith Frey, Winnipeg, Manitoba; mission agency administrator.

Linda Caldwell Fuller, Americus, Georgia; co-founder, Habitat for Humanity.

Millard Fuller, Americus Georgia; attorney/business and mission agency executive.

Sandra Graham, Greenville, South Carolina; mission agency administrator.

Stanley W. Green, Elkhart, Indiana; mission agency executive.

Bruce Gunter, Atlanta, Georgia; business executive.

Nancy R. Heisey, Barto, Pennsylvania; college professor.

Linda Helmus, Lancaster, Pennsylvania; teacher; seminary student.

Anna Juhnke, North Newton, Kansas; college professor.

Gerald Kaufman, Akron, Pennsylvania; family counselor.

James M. Lapp, Sellersville, Pennsylvania; pastor; church executive.

Jonathan P. Larson, Atlanta, Georgia; pastor.

Earl Martin, Harrisonburg, Virginia; writer/mission agency administrator.

Wilmer Martin, Waterloo, Ontario; pastor; mission agency executive.

Ron Mathies, Ephrata, Pennsylvania; relief agency executive.

Betsy Headrick McCrae, Hanoi, Vietnam; mission agency administrator.

Lynette Meck, Akron, Pennsylvania; human resources administrator.

Larry W. Nikkel, Wichita, Kansas; church agency/college executive.

Juana F. Nuñez, Ocoee, Florida; Bible teacher/minister.

Leona Dueck Penner, Winnipeg, Manitoba; writer/mission agency administrator.

Vern Preheim, North Newton, Kansas; retired church executive.

Jim Purks, Americus, Georgia; writer.

Vera Randall, Dural Australia; business executive.

Lance Renault, Greenville, South Carolina; mission agency administrator.

David Johnson Rowe, Pittsfield, Massachusetts; pastor.

Warren Sawyer, Swampscott, Massachusetts; business/church agency executive.

Paul Schrag, Newton, Kansas; writer/editor.

Linda Shelly, Lancaster, Pennsylvania; relief agency administrator.

Wilbert R. Shenk, Pasadena, California; seminary professor/ mission agency executive.

Richard Showalter, Salunga, Pennsylvania; mission agency executive.

Stuart W. Showalter, Goshen, Indiana; college professor.

Ben Sprunger, Washington, Ohio; college/business executive.

Edgar Stoesz, Akron, Pennsylvania; mission/business executive.

John K. Stoner, Akron, Pennsylvania; pastor/college professor.

Carol Suter, Kansas City, Missouri; attorney/business executive.

Ted Swisher, Americus, Georgia; mission agency administrator.

W. Clyde Tilley, Seymour, Tennessee; seminary professor/pastor.

Mel West, Columbia, Missouri; pastor/mission entrepreneur.

David Wine, Abilene, Kansas; pastor; business/church executive.

June Alliman Yoder, Elkhart, Indiana; seminary/college professor.

More Meditations for Meetings

If you have prepared a meditation for a meeting (or plan to do so) and would like to have it considered for a possible second volume of *Meditations for Meetings*, please submit it to Edgar Stoesz, 929 Broad Street, Akron, PA 17501.

Please include the following elements:

1) A scripture passage of 3-5 verses, using whatever version you prefer.

2) A story from life so that the theme has energy and a point at which an audience can connect.

3) A few paragraphs of commentary.

4) A prayer.

5) A summary thought of 1-2 lines.

Maximum length is 450 words. Avoid sermonizing and obtuse theological language. The audience is a board, a small gathering of men and women, or a leader preparing to give direction to a board or committee. The intent of each meditation is to make God's presence more consciously felt in the small group, gathered to do a common task.

About the Editor

Edgar Stoesz has spent many hours in meetings where he has heard countless meditations and led some, as well.

He was a staff member of Mennonite Central Committee for 33 years, seven of those years as Associate Executive Secretary. He served as President-CEO of Mennonite Indemnity for 14 years. Stoesz spent six years on the board of Habitat for Humanity International, four of those years as Chair. He is currently First Vice President of Hospital Albert Schweitzer (Haiti). Presently he also chairs the board of the American Leprosy Mission.

He is the co-author of the book *Doing Good Better: How to Be an Effective Board Member of a Nonprofit Organization* (Good Books, 1997). He has written extensively for church periodicals and organizational newsletters.